CHRISTIAN ANSWERS

TO

YOUR QUESTIONS

VOLUME 2

Gerard Desrochers
Redemptorist

ISBN 2-89238-313-7
Imprimi potest
Guy Pilote
Provincial of Redemptorists
Saint Anne de Beaupre, 2001

Printed in Canada
Imprimé au Canada

My gratitude to all those who helped me so generously in the preparation of this book.

My sincere thanks to my confreres for their precious advices, particularly to Father Maurice Dionne who revised carefully the whole text.

I am deeply grateful to Therese Albert, to my nephew John Svab and to my niece Margaret Svab Burton, who translated all the questions and answers. My niece Margaret edited the whole book with so much attention and efficacy. May God bless them all!

TABLE OF CONTENTS

X – SAINTS AND ANGELS

XI – FAITH

XII – CHRISTIAN LIFE

XIII – ECUMENISM

XIV – SOCIAL LIFE

XV – SEXUALITY

XVI – BIOETHICS AND MORAL PROBLEMS

XVII – DEATH, THE HEREAFTER

PREFACE

"Yahweh gave our ancestors strict orders
to teach it to their children;
the next generation was to learn it,
the children still to be born,

and these in their turn to tell their own children
so that they too would put their confidence in God..."

You hold in your hands Father Desrochers' latest book: *Christian Answers to Your Questions – Volume 2*. We might take the words of Psalm 78, quoted above, and compare this work to a 'child' that has been 'born' to teach and communicate hope.

Based on Holy Scripture and Church Tradition, these pages strive very simply to answer current concerns and pragmatic questions of our society, which, in light of human, social and technological development, are in constant need of clarification.

Father Desrochers presents Gospel-based answers to the questions of contemporary Christians. In the spirit of Saint Alphonsus of Liguori, the founder of the Congregation of the Most Holy Redeemer, Father Desrochers renders God's Word more accessible, in an attempt to transmit hope-filled answers to a new generation.

Christian Answers to Your Questions – Volume 2 is not a systematic doctrinal treatise. Rather, it is meant to be kept within easy reach on your shelf, to be used frequently as a reference text and inspirational tool. I sincerely hope that it will guide you as you journey with confidence through God's mysterious ways and that it will give you the courage to advance steadily on the bright road mapped out for you towards eternity.

Guy Pilote, C.Ss.R.
Provincial Superior

- I -

GOD

Existence
The Trinity
Jesus
The Holy Spirit

IS THERE A GOD?

* * *

"Does God exist?"... "I don't know", you may answer. Yet, it is important to know. Life has a different sense and meaning if there is a God who created the world, who saved the world, a God who commands the night and day. Life is not the same if we believe in God.

Without God, our existence here on earth would be meaningless! What's the use of living if there is no God, if there is no afterlife, if we only live 'for the moment' in a world full of injustice, violence and suffering? If this were the case, wouldn't it be better to end our lives as early as possible? What's the use of spending our lives in such disappointment and wretchedness if God does not exist?

Each one of us encounters God, particularly in those moments of unexpected joy or sorrow.

We know that God exists by our natural reasoning and by divine faith. Even in the absence of faith, our intuition, unless we ignore it, will attest to his existence. How can we deny his existence when in the silence of the night we wonder at all the stars in the heavens above? When we stand before a magnificent landscape composed of mountains, plains and rivers, can we really attribute all this to chance? When a child is born, when a baby smiles for the first time, isn't this enough to believe that there is a Creator of life? When we marvel at the complex and delicate organism that is our human body, complete with a curiosity and thirst for knowledge, can we still doubt the existence of a God who fashioned our bodies and souls?

So many things speak to me of God if I am still, if I contemplate and reflect. Unless we hold "truth imprisoned", as Saint Paul writes (Rm 1: 18-20)! The extravagances of life and sin keep me from God and tempt me to doubt. But God does exist!

All human beings, in all ages, think of God and yearn for God... From the depths of all hearts, there is a yearning for God, a taste of eternity.

What my reasoning allows me to discover, revelation makes it a certitude: God exists!

Throughout the Old Testament, before the coming of Christ, God spoke and revealed himself. Since Adam and Eve, then Abraham, Moses and all the prophets, during the exodus of the Hebrew people, God manifested himself. He delivered his message. He allied himself with humans. The Providence of the Lord was at work.

Then, two thousand years later, Jesus came, Son of Mary, Son of God.

As I listen to the Gospel of salvation for all, as I hear the Good News that we are saved and God's children, as I see proofs of his goodness, of his mercy, of his concern for children, the poor and sinners, as I see his dying for us and rising from the dead, I have evidence that God is among us, a God full of tenderness, a God who loves us personally.

I believe in God. I know him by his works; I also know him because he has revealed himself to me.

My life makes complete sense because God exists. Because God exists, I know that good will conquer evil, that life will win over death, that at the resurrection I will live forever in the abundance of happiness. I have only to accept Jesus and walk along his road. He is "the Way" (Jn 14: 6).

God exists. This is my faith!

Reasoning and faith assure me of his existence. In his encyclical *Faith and Reason*, Pope John Paul II declared: "Faith and reason are like two wings that permit the human spirit to rise toward contemplation of the truth". The pope reasserts the importance of reason. Philosophy is important for the intelligence of faith, but revealed truths must not be forgotten.

Without reason, says the Pope, there is danger of agnosticism. According to agnostics, we can never know the origin or the destiny of things. Without reason, faith becomes fideism, only sentimentality. Yes, reason, as well as faith, has me convinced that God does indeed exist!

WHAT'S THE MEANING OF THE TRINITY?

* * *

Trinity means one God in three Persons.

In our Christian faith we adore the Trinity. This is the most precious dogma of our Christian faith, the central mystery of God and of Christian life. "The faith of all Christians rests on the Trinity", proclaimed Saint Caesarius of Arles, the apostle of the Frankish Church, who died in 543. God is One and Triune. There is but one God in three distinct Persons: the Father, the Son and the Holy Spirit. We proclaim our trinitarian faith when we make the sign of the cross "in the name of the Father, and of the Son and of the Holy Spirit". We praise him when we say: "Glory be to the Father and to the Son and to the Holy Spirit".

This basic article of our faith is obscure in the Old Testament, but was explicitly taught by Jesus. Christ often told his listeners that God was his Father, to the point of being accused of blasphemy and put to death. He prompted us to consider God as our own Father and ourselves as his heirs. He also revealed the salutary presence of the Holy Spirit and added that it was for our own good that he himself was going because unless he went, the Holy Spirit, the Advocate, would not come to us (Jn 16: 7).

Early in her history, the Church did her best to formulate in clear terms this sacred mystery of the Trinity. She did so at the council of Nicaea in 325 and at the first council of Constantinople in 381. Since her origin, the Church has requested new Christians to profess their faith in the Trinity at the moment of baptism (*Catechism of the Catholic Church*, No 232 ss).

Saint Paul is adamant: "God sent his Son... to enable us to be adopted as sons... God has sent the Spirit of his Son into our hearts..., the Spirit that cries 'Abba, Father'" (Ga 4: 4-6). Saint Paul turned to the Trinity for blessings: "The grace of the Lord Jesus Christ, the love of God and the fellowship of the Holy Spirit be with you all" (2 Co 13: 13), a prayer which is still the priest's greeting at the beginning of Mass. It is an homage to the Trinity.

CAN WE PROVE THE EXISTENCE OF THE TRINITY?

It's hard for me to believe in the Trinity, especially since I received the visit of a Jehovah's Witness who explained to me that neither the Bible nor Jesus mention the Trinity.

Is there a written proof about the Trinity?

* * *

I sincerely hope that you will read the *Catechism of the Catholic Church*, a book which is complete and easy to read; it explains our Christian and Catholic faith. You can buy it in Catholic bookstores.

In it is written: "The mystery of the Most Holy Trinity is the central mystery of Christian faith and life. It is the mystery of God in himself. It is therefore the source of all the other mysteries of faith, the light that enlightens them. It is the most fundamental and essential teaching in the 'hierarchy of the truths of faith'" (No 234). We have an understanding of this mystery thanks to God's revelation.

In many sections of the Bible, Jesus reveals God his Father to us: Father as Creator; Father in relation to his unique Son, Jesus Christ; Father in relation to us as his adoptive children. There are numerous quotations; for example: Jn 5, Jn 17. Here is a passage from Saint Matthew: "Everything has been entrusted to me by my Father; and no one knows the Son except the Father, just as no one knows the Father except the Son and those to whom the Son chooses to reveal him" (Mt 11: 27).

Jesus also spoke of the Holy Spirit, the other Paraclete. We read in Saint John: "When the Spirit of truth comes he will lead you to the complete truth" (Jn 16: 13ss).

The Trinity is one. There is but one God in three Persons. These Persons are distinct, yet, linked together. If there are three Persons, there is only one divinity. This mystery lies beyond our reason; it comes within the competence of our faith thanks to God's revelation.

Through baptism required by Jesus, a baptism conferred "in the name of the Father and of the Son and of the Holy Spirit", we share the life of the Trinity. Let's listen to Jesus who gave this order to his disciples: "Go, therefore, make disciples of all the nations; baptize them in the name of the Father and of the Son and of the Holy Spirit" (Mt 28: 19).

Our Catholic faith in the Trinity is shared by Orthodox, Anglicans and Protestants.

The Pope says: "There is no *tritheism*, no three Gods. Unicity in God is expressed in the mystery of the three divine Persons..., a mystery human reason cannot explain, but which we can accept from what is divinely revealed concerning the intimate nature of God" (May 5, 1999).

HOW CAN WE RECONCILE LOVE AND JUSTICE IN GOD?

God is love; he is also justice. Love and justice are united. What is the justice of God? Why isn't it talked about anymore?

* * *

Justice and love are two of the attributes of God. It is our way of expressing it, to compartmentalize..., but in God all is perfect and unified.

Why do we not talk anymore of justice? It is because another word for the justice of God is mercy.

To save us, he "emptied himself to assume the condition of a slave, and became as men are...; he was humbler yet, even to accepting death, death on a cross" (Ph 2: 7-8).

Because of love! And this is the Good News, the reason for our faith, the source of our hope, the food of our love!

God is revealed in Jesus. This just God is called "Love" (1 Jn 4: 8). Love has become incarnate in Jesus, Love which nourishes our life! His religion is a religion of love, not simply a series of oppressive laws. The commandments of God pave the true way to happiness.

Love drives away fear.

Let us ponder the consoling words of the Bible: "Everyone moved by the Spirit is a son of God. The spirit you received is not the spirit of slaves bringing fear into your lives again; it is the spirit of sons, and it makes us cry out, 'Abba, Father!'" (Rm 8: 14-15).

If I dream of the justice of God, it isn't with the fear of a servant, it is with the trust of a child who feels loved by his Father in heaven, by a God who is infinitely good.

We can talk of the justice of God; it exists. But we can also talk of the love of God. As children of God, is it not our preference?

IS JESUS GOD?

* * *

Yes, he is!

In the 4th century, the Church was greatly challenged by Arianism. Arius, a priest in Alexandria, taught that Jesus, the 'Logos', the Word of God, was not God, but a creature of God.

His heresy denied the true divinity of Christ. The heresy spread throughout the Roman Empire. The first ecumenical council, the

Council of Nicaea, in 325, affirmed the Christian faith in the divinity of Jesus. It declared the consubstantiality of the Father and the Son. The divinity of Jesus does not come from an adoption by the Father. Saint John tells us: "In the beginning was the Word: and the Word was with God and the Word was God... The Word was made flesh, he lived among us..." (Jn 1: 1-3, 14). Later, in 381, at the first Council of Constantinople, the divinity of the Holy Spirit received similar authoritative definition.

The heresy of the Arians was supported by the emperors of the time. Saint Athanasius, defender of the faith, was exiled five times for speaking against the heresy. Among other heroes of the true faith we find the popes, Saint Hilary of Poitiers, and the Cappadocians: Saint Basil the Great, Saint Gregory of Nazianzus and Saint Gregory of Nyssa. Arianism disappeared late in the 5th century.

Jesus Christ is God; we proclaim this in our Creed. In him there is only one person who is divine, as it was affirmed at the Council of Ephesus in 431, but there are two natures, one human and one divine, as it was defined at the Council of Chalcedon in 451. The two natures can never be confused, can never be mixed up; they exist in harmony within the divine person of the Word.

In the Gospels, Jesus speaks at times according to his *human* nature to explain that the Father is greater than he is (Jn 14: 28). In other places he speaks according to his *divine* nature to assert that he and his Father are one (Jn 10: 30).

DID JESUS KNOW THAT HE WAS GOD?

In his science or human conscience, acquired or infuse, did Jesus know that he was God? Was he aware of his divinity?...

* * *

This delicate question has been debated by the exegetes.

The Tradition of the Church, its pastors, the Fathers of the Church, theologians and simple faithful all answer yes to the question: Jesus knew that he was God! Jesus could not ignore his divine nature. He spoke often of his Father in heaven. There are many examples in Scripture, especially in the Gospel of Saint John, where Jesus revealed his knowledge of his divinity: "Everything has been entrusted to me by my Father" (Mt 11: 27); "Abba (Father)!" he said (Mk 14: 36); "Father, forgive them" (Lk 23: 34); "Whoever refuses honor to the Son refuses honor to the Father who sent him" (Jn 5: 23); "If you did know me, you would know my Father as well" (Jn 8: 19); "The Father and I are one" (Jn 10: 30); "The Father is in me and I am in the Father" (Jn 10: 38); "To have seen me is to have seen the Father" (Jn 14: 9); "Everything the Father has is mine" (Jn 16: 15); "He spoke of God as his own Father and so made himself God's equal" (Jn 5: 18); etc.

All of the texts cited above and many others answer in the affirmative, because they are human words that come directly from the mouth of Jesus and are passed on to us through his human nature. *How* Jesus knew in his human nature that he was God is more difficult to explain.

I repeat that the original question asks whether Jesus was conscious or not of his divinity. The question is not whether Jesus was divine; we believe firmly that he was. If nowadays non-Christians compare him with some great people such as Moses, Buddha and Confucius, they are forgetting the essential difference between these historical figures and Jesus: Jesus is God. Faithful to the whole Tradition, we can further explain that he was aware of his divinity, that he affirmed it through his words, that he acted as God during his life.

Millions of people have died as martyrs, millions of religious men and women lived in cloistered monasteries, thousands of missionaries sailed across oceans, Christians everywhere keep living according to the Gospels: the reason is that they believed and still believe in the divinity of Jesus and in what he said.

2000 years ago, Jesus, in full knowledge of his divinity as the Son of God, as God, proclaimed himself equal to God and was killed because of it. His resurrection proved that he spoke the truth in believing himself to be God.

IS JESUS WHITE OR BLACK?

* * *

This question was asked by a Black.

Behind this question, I detect the suffering of someone who has experienced racism, who is oppressed because of the colour of his skin.

God became incarnate, one of us. He was born into a human family, that of Mary and Joseph, in a corner of the world known today as the Holy Land. He was a Jew called Jesus.

He came to save humans, regardless of race or colour of skin. His religion is universal and transcends all cultural barriers.

We may say that Jesus is neither a white man nor a colored person; he is the God of all humankind.

In reality, we, his disciples, who are we? Do we truly try to imitate him? Discrimination has not disappeared from our society. There is still some fascism or neo-fascism in our hearts. Blacks, natives, Jews and immigrants of diverse ethnic origins all encounter prejudice and persecution from such attitudes.

Saint Paul teaches us: "There is no room for distinction between Greek and Jew, between the circumcised or the uncircumcised, or between barbarian and Scythian, slave and free man. There is only Christ: he is everything and he is in everything" (Col 3: 11). We are all brothers and sisters, children of the same heavenly Father.

WHEN WAS THE HOLY SPIRIT FIRST RECOGNIZED?

There are many references to the Holy Spirit in the Bible, even in the Old Testament. When was he first recognized as the Third Person of the Trinity? When was this dogma first proclaimed by the Church? How can I be sure that it is the Holy Spirit that is guiding me?

* * *

Basing herself on Christ's teaching, the Church always believed in the divinity of the Holy Spirit. There are numerous references to the Holy Spirit in the Gospels. For example: "Go, therefore, make disciples of all the nations; baptize them in the name of the Father and of the Son and of the Holy Spirit" (Mt 28: 19); "The Advocate, the Holy Spirit, whom the Father will send in my name, will teach you everything..." (Jn 14: 26); "When the Advocate comes,... the Spirit of truth who issues from the Father, he will be my witness" (Jn 15: 26); "He breathed on them and said: 'Receive the Holy Spirit'" (Jn 20: 22); etc.

The Lord's doctrine had to be clearly defined to be better understood. It needed to be expressed theologically. During the first centuries, the Church had to respond to heretics who proclaimed their errors in loud voices, often with the support of the emperors. The fourth and the fifth centuries, especially in the Middle East, were periods of doctrinal crises: christological and trinitarian, in other words concerning the Lord Jesus and the divine Trinity.

At the Council of Nicaea (325), the divinity of Christ was solemnly defined to refute the Arian heresy. At the Council of Constantinople (381), the doctrine of Nicaea was reaffirmed and the Fathers of the Council defined as a dogma the divinity of the Holy Spirit, already the faith of true Christians.

From the time of the Apostles, Christians have recited the Creed: "I believe in God, the Father Almighty..., in Jesus Christ his only Son..., in the Holy Spirit!". We cannot truly call ourselves Christians without believing in God, Father, Son and Spirit.

The criteria for discernment are clear: true charity, the doctrine of Christ and his Church, and good fruits, especially the fruits of the Spirit that are love, peace and joy (Ga: 5: 22).

CAN SAINT ANNE INTERCEDE FOR ME WITH DIVINE ENERGY?

I ask Saint Anne to intercede for me with divine Energy, to obtain a cure for my sickness.

Even though I know that the solution of my problem and the cure of my healing are within me, I ask for her support. Am I not justified?

* * *

I praise you for your faith and your devotion to Saint Anne, the Virgin Mary's mother and Jesus' grandmother. At the Shrine of Saint Anne de Beaupre, crowds of pilgrims come every day to ask for her powerful and kind intercession; she is rightly called 'Good' Saint Anne.

Still, I am puzzled by your prayer.

When you wrote about God, you wrote about divine Energy. That is New Age terminology and is ambiguous. Those of us who have faith call God our Father, according to Holy Scripture (Mt 6: 9). To all who accept Jesus as their Savior, "he gave power to become children of God" (Jn 1: 12). We are right when we call him our Father.

God is our Father; he is not an energy, divine or cosmic, to which we want to be harmoniously united. Our revealed religion is so much richer, more beautiful, more consoling than the vague and abstract deism of the New Age.

The New Age movement goes back to the sixties, at the time of the hippies; people then believed that the world would be renewed.

They thought that the New Age would be a turning point toward peace and happiness. The age of Aquarius would replace the age of Pisces (the Christian era). For those who believe in the New Age, there is but one reality: the Energy; they say it gives life to everything. We are to merge with the cosmic and divine Energy. We can improve our human potential through techniques and knowledge: esoterism, gnosis, spiritism, ecology and oriental religions (reincarnation, etc.).

Instead of being influenced by the New Age Movement, we have only to read the Bible to know who God is and to find out who we really are.

Is it true to say: "I know that the solution to my problem is within me"? Yes and no. Yes, if you mean that you can do something to make yourself better, with the help of the Lord. No, if you are implying that you alone can help yourself.

The New Age, with its cult of 'self', rather than of God, often exerts its influence on us without our knowing it. We can easily fall into that ancient heresy, pelagianism, if we believe that we can do everything by ourselves, apart from divine grace. In Europe, there are those who speak of the Next Age which will stress even more individualism, the 'ego'. We must beware.

Keep praying to the Lord with the help of Saint Anne. Believe in a personal God. Find out more about how God, our Father. Jesus said: "You should pray like this: Our Father in heaven..." (Mt 6: 9). He will look after you. Do not worry (Mt 6 : 30: 34).

- II -

THE BIBLE

Interpretation
Fundamentalism
Commandments

CAN YOU TELL ME ABOUT THE BIBLE?

* * *

It is very important for all Christians to study and understand the Holy Bible.

The Bible is made up of 73 books, 46 for the Old Testament and 27 for the New Testament. The New Testament is hidden in the Old and the Old becomes clear in the New.

The Holy Scripture is God's Word written in the Bible. In the sacred books, God speaks to us. God's Word gives strength to the Church and nourishes the soul (Vatican II, *The Divine Revelation*, No 21).

With the help of the Holy Spirit, let's give God's Word "the obedience of faith" (Rm 16: 26). "If you make my Word your home you will indeed be my disciples", Jesus says (Jn 8: 31).

The Bible is a history book and, throughout history, through Abraham, Moses, David, the prophets, etc., God revealed his love for us. We respect the Bible, the timeless bestseller, and its message is vital for you and me. The Sacred Scriptures testify to Jesus (Jn 5: 39). "They are the basis and the pillar of our faith", wrote Saint Irenaeus. Saint Jerome added: "To ignore the Scriptures is to ignore Christ". We must prayerfully read the Bible, make it a *lectio divina*, especially the New Testament, and above all the Gospels.

"All Scripture is inspired by God", wrote Saint Paul to his disciple Timothy (2 Tm 3: 16). God is the Author of the Bible, but each sacred writer wrote with his formation, his temperament and style. The Bible is God's Word; it is also human word! There is no danger of doctrinal errors in the Bible, in regard to faith and morals. It is God teaching us, offering his salvation.

We must never forget the primary importance of the Word of God: it is a fire (Jr 23: 29), a light (Ps 119: 130), the truth (Jn 17: 17), and it is life (Heb 4: 12). May it produce its crop, a hundredfold, sixty, or thirty (Mt 13: 8). Our knowledge must not be restricted to a few selected passages. Listen to God's Word (Jn 8: 47), observe it (Lk 6: 47) and spread it (2 Tm 4: 1-5).

Like the disciples of Emmaus, may our hearts burn within us as we listen to God's Word (Lk 24: 32).

IS IT WRONG TO INTERPRET THE BIBLE?

* * *

All Christian heresies sprout from false interpretations of the Bible. A sound interpretation of Holy Scripture is a must. And, according to her Founder, Jesus, it is the Church's responsibility to provide it. The scientific study of Holy Scripture is called hermeneutics or exegesis. Images, symbols and literary genres used in the Bible must be well understood. To properly interpret the words of Scripture, we must be aware of the context, we must grasp the full message of the Bible and of the Church's Tradition. The use of a well-translated Bible is also very important.

I referred in the above paragraph to the Tradition of the Church... The apostles passed on the teaching they had received and, after their death, others continued the Tradition (2 Tm 2: 2. 14), always through the inspiration of the Holy Spirit. Together, "Sacred Tradition and Sacred Scripture form one sacred deposit of the Word of God, which is committed to the Church" (*Divine Revelation*, No 10). They cannot be separated. We need to mention here the authority of the Church, that of the Pope and bishops, successors of the apostles; they alone are authorized to give the authentic interpretation of God's Word. They are the pastors to whom Christ has entrusted his Church. We cannot separate the Holy Scriptures, the Tradition and the official authority of the Church.

WHAT IS THE MEANING OF FUNDAMENTALISM?

* * *

Biblical fundamentalism, always the source of great controversy, consists of a literal interpretation of the Sacred Scriptures. It implies the complete refusal of ecumenism. It is 'fundamental', claim its followers, especially some American Protestant religions. Fundamentalism is also found in some interpretations of the Koran.

These days, fundamentalism makes headlines, especially Muslim fundamentalism in countries such as Pakistan, Sudan, Egypt, Nigeria and elsewhere. The Ayatollah Khomeini imposed a fundamentalist political party after winning the Iranian revolution in 1979.

Bishop John Joseph, writing specifically about Islamic fundamentalism, states that fundamentalists refuse to compromise on anything, and believe themselves to be the sole possessors of the truth; they would die for their beliefs. Based on their emotions, fanatical ideas, and a morbid fear of modernization and secularism, they attempt to impose their religious ideas even to the point of using violence. Terrorism, beatings, amputations and massacres occur frequently in some Muslim countries.

I write here not about the Islamic world in general, but of 'militant Islamic groups'. Iman Khomeini, in a *'fatwa'* or religious decree, condemned the writer Salmon Rushdie to death because he accused him of blasphemy against Allah. A group of *'fatwas'* form the *'charia'*, the canonical Islamic law. Religious minorities, women and intellectuals suffer from these laws in Islamic states.

"Every type of discrimination... is to be overcome and eradicated as contrary to God's intent" (*Gaudium et Spes*, No 29). The Universal Declaration of Human Rights, proclaimed in 1948, continues to be ignored in many parts of the world.

Properly understood, Islam promotes peace, respect and tolerance. It defends family values, so too does the Church. Dialogue is desirable with this tolerant Islam, especially so as Muslims increase in number within our Christian societies.

Uncompromising fundamentalism and disrespectful proselytism can infiltrate all religions, and mocks the God who himself respects the freedom of all those he created in love.

DO GOD'S COMMANDMENTS STILL EXIST?

* * *

Certainly, they exist!

They are found in the Bible, in the Holy Scriptures, in the Word of God that spans the limits of space and time (Ex 20: 2-17; Dt 5: 6-21).

Remember the commandments that the Lord Yahweh gave to Moses in the Old Testament. It is a Decalogue, ten statements. They are summarized below:

You shall not put other gods before me...

You shall not falsely use the name of Yahweh your God...

You shall remember the Sabbath day and keep it holy...

Honor your father and your mother...

Do not kill...

Do not commit adultery...

Do not steal...

Do not give false witness against your neighbor...

Do not covet your neighbor's house...

Do not covet your neighbor's spouse...

The Decalogue outlines the way of life with which to align oneself with God. The commandments of God never change and carry serious obligations for living. The first three commandments have to do with the love of God; the other seven are for the love of neighbor.

When Jesus was alive, he did not abolish the law, rather he brought the law to perfection (Mt 5:17). He reiterated the commandments, all the while insisting that the greatest and first commandment is the love for the Lord our God, adding, after that, love for neighbor (Mt 22: 37-40). He demanded not only the exterior practice of the commandments, but that they be taken to heart, with an interior disposition that would respect the law in a spirit of love.

To understand God's commandments, it is necessary to read Jesus' *Sermon on the Mount*. Listen to his teachings on the Beatitudes. Jesus outlines the road to happiness. He invites everyone, not only to follow God's commandments, but also to go beyond them. We must obey the commandments, but we must also have hearts that are poor in spirit, full of gentleness, strong in affliction, thirsting for justice, merciful and pure. We must be peacemakers, even to the point of suffering persecution in our struggle for justice (Mt 5: 2-12; Lk 6: 20-23).

Jesus is not against the commandments transmitted to Moses. He helps us to understand their importance, value and significance.

To better grasp God's commandments, we should look at how Jesus lived. Jesus followed the Ten Commandments; Jesus practiced the Beatitudes.

We should read God's commandments carefully now that there is so much disrespect for God, the preservation of life and human dignity.

Pope John Paul II wrote, in his Apostolic Letter on the *Day of the Lord*, that the Sabbath, Sunday for Christians, must be kept holy. Every commandment of God remains relevant, more than ever.

There are also commandments of the Church. It is with her commandments and laws that the Church helps us to follow the commandments of God.

The Church may modify her commandments; she can never change the commandments of God.

DON'T YOU THINK THAT THERE ARE ERRORS IN SAINT PAUL'S WRITINGS?

Saint Paul is not Jesus. There are errors in what he wrote, doctrines contrary to Jesus' teaching. For example, he told women to be silent, which is anti-Christian. Jesus never said anything specific concerning how men and women should dress.

* * *

I can't agree with your statement: there is no contradiction between the inspired doctrine of Saint Paul and that of Jesus. Saint Paul's letters are part of the Bible, of Holy Scripture. There is no doctrinal inconsistency between Paul's teaching and Jesus' teaching.

However, we can say that the writings of Saint Paul contain detailed codes of behavior that belonged to the culture of his time. There is a difference between a doctrine and a discipline of life.

It is similar today... We do not change the Church or her doctrine when we update certain disciplinary obligations: nowadays Mass is in the vernacular, communion is given on the tongue or in the hand, there is a relaxation of the Eucharistic fast, etc.

Saint Paul instructed the followers of Jesus to observe a certain custom and behavior appropriate to the period in which he lived: silence for women, covering the head, etc., which was in no way contrary to the teaching of Christ: love for God and neighbor, authentic faith, moral conduct according to God's laws, etc. He also taught that all were equal before God (Ga 3: 28) and that a man should love his wife as Christ loved the Church (I Co 5: 25). We find in Saint Paul, the great Apostle, an exceptional wealth of doctrine. We nourish our faith with his teaching, which is authentically Christian.

WHAT IS THE MEANING OF 666 IN THE APOCALYPSE?

I have never found the answers I seek regarding specific texts of the Apocalyse, Rv 13: 16-18 and 14: 9-11:

"...If anyone is clever enough, he may interpret the number of the beast: it is the number of a man, the number is 666"; "...And the smoke of their torture will go up forever and ever. There will be no respite, night or day, for those who worshiped the beast or its statue or accepted branding with its name".

* * *

I cannot give you a completely satisfactory answer here without saying that the explanation of the whole Apocalypse, not only the two passages in question, is a bit complicated because of the liberal use of symbols and imagery.

The Apocalypse, a word of Greek origin, means 'revelation'. It is God's revelation of hidden things, particularly with respect to the future. The sacred writer received these revelations as visions. It is not so much the visions themselves that are of value, but what their symbolism represents: numbers, things, people, etc... It is easy to get confused. Similar revelations are the Old Testament visions of Ezekiel and Daniel, who wrote during times of hardship to reaffirm faith in Yahweh.

To properly understand the Apocalypse, one has to remember that they were written to reassure Christians who were suffering persecution at the time.

Saint John, the author of the Apocalypse, wrote about the time of hard persecution by the Roman Empire (the Beast), under the instigation of Satan. John tells of a vision from God where the Lamb is given a decree against the persecutors. There will be tragedies, but the faithful will be protected. The scourge will pass among them for the conversion of hearts. But, Rome, the Beast, the Babylon, will be destroyed. Afterwards, there will come a time of prosperity for the Church of Christ, followed by a new assault by Satan. Then the final reign of our glorious Savior will come.

The Book of Revelation, the Apocalypse, is a book of hope. God lives among his people. The Church will survive in spite of all suffering.

It is in this context that the passages mentioned in the question should be interpreted, especially the number of the Beast, the Antichrist: 666 (also 616). The *Jerusalem Bible* states that, in Greek as well as in Hebrew, 'each letter had a numeric value depending on its place in the alphabet. The number of a name is the total sum of its letters. In this case, '666' would be Nero Caesar (in Hebrew letters). It would appear that he would be the one represented by this "number of a man" (Rv 13: 18). This explanation seems plausible.

A lot of ink has been used in the effort to interpret this number, sometimes by those who are not well qualified and who are inclined to dwell on fantasy. The first Christians in Asia, who could have told us about this number of man, understood more fully what John was alluding to. By writing a little bit obscurely for the local pagans, John avoided increased persecution. For example, he substituted the name of Rome with the name of Babylon. Unfortunately the first Christians didn't leave us their explanations of the number that contained so much warning. The number 6, which represented something that was incomplete (7 minus 1), revealed also that the reign of the Beast would not succeed, and that Christians should remain hopeful.

The Apocalypse is a message of hope to all believers in a time of severe persecution against the Church.

- III -

LIFE

Meaning
Changes
The education of children

DOES LIFE HAVE ANY MEANING?

* * *

I see damaging forces at work in the world. I see the forces of power and evil that cannot be apparently contained or mastered! People live in extreme misery, are deprived of freedom, are simply destroyed. So many children are murdered even before they are born; others are malnourished and die of hunger. The elderly fade away in solitude and uselessness; will they be helpless victims of euthanasia?

Wars continue to be a threat and conflicts break out as easily as a bush fire. And the horrors of war include torture, violence, deportation and death.

Does life make any sense? For many people, it means only a slow death, an agony that never ends. To be born, to suffer, to have hearts betrayed and broken, to labor simply to find food and shelter, then to disappear... Does life really have any meaning?

We must never doubt!

Life, especially human life, knows its seasons. The gloom of autumn and the cold of winter are replaced with a living spring and an enchanted summer. Even though there is often rain and even hail in life, there are also rays of sunshine.

However, the highs that alternate with the lows, the return of health after an illness, prosperity, or the happiness of loved ones, these are not the true reasons that give my life meaning. I uncover the true sense of life by the grace of my faith.

The Lord Jesus tells us not to worry about our earthly life (Mt 6: 25).

In my faith, I believe that life is the greatest gift I have ever received. Life comes from God. He is "the source of all life" (1 Tm 6: 13). He is the "fountain of life" (Ps 36:10). My life is a participation in the life of God. Life on earth continues into eternal life. My human life allows me a foretaste of eternal happiness.

This is the will of the Creator, our God. His love exploded into life. And he saw that it was "very good" (Gn 1: 31). Even though our first parents disobeyed God, wanted to travel a road far away from God, in their darkest moments God came to their rescue. He offered them light. He promised a Redeemer. He sent his only Son to save us. "God loved us with so much love that he was generous with his mercy: when we were dead through our sins he brought us to life with Christ" (Ep 2: 5).

When Jesus came, he proclaimed: "I have come so that they may have life and have it to the full" (Jn 10: 10). He gave up his life for us (1 Jn 3: 16). He is the Life (Jn 14: 6).

By the grace of our Lord and Savior, life is always worth living. Because the Lord is present in our lives to help us. He does not leave us orphans; he promised (Jn 14: 18). Trust in him! He has placed brothers and sisters along the road to guide us and to assist us. There have always been earthly angels, even today.

Jesus preached the Good News that we are children of God, heirs of heaven and coheirs with Christ (Rm 8: 17). Our suffering, united with his, will yield eternal happiness. Our faith tells us this (2 Co 4: 17). We always have hope despite the storms of life.

My earthly life, so limited, so easily ended, will one day be transformed by God who loves me personally and with eternal love. I place all my hope in him; I will not be shaken. I want to believe "against all hope" (Rm 4: 18). I will not be disappointed in my Christian trust (1 P 2: 6).

Life, what a great gift from God! Life means hope, joy and love for all who discover God! Everyone who believes in Jesus has eternal life (Jn 3: 16). One day there will be no more tears or sadness; the world of the past will be gone (Rv 21: 4).

I believe in life because I believe in God who gives us life and who is the Master of life.

WHY HAS LIFE CHANGED SO MUCH?

Why has life changed so much? Or better still, why does it never seem to change?

* * *

Yes, you are correct in stating, with apparent contradiction, that life changes and yet it stays the same.

"...And there is nothing new under the sun," Qoheleth laments nostalgically (Qo 1: 9). "This, too, is vanity and chasing of the wind" (Qo 4: 4).

When we examine the information given to us through the mass media, we see that humanity is pretty much the same as always, with wars, genocides, ungodliness and immorality. There is even an apparent resurgence of the forces of evil, with increasing abortion, euthanasia, with drug epidemics and the consequences of increased substance abuse. Young people revolt and their parents are worried. Multinationals hold third world nations in financial bondage. We receive somber reports such as these on a daily basis, with a few local sensationalist stories added for flavor.

At the same time, humanity, according to God's plan, attempts as it were "to conquer the earth and creation" (Gn 1: 28). Scientific techniques develop and improve; space crafts become more and more capable of exploring the universe. People, masses of ordinary people, remain essentially good, seeking a good life, love and happiness, working for the wellbeing of their children. Evidence of this goodness is apparent especially in times of disaster. Spiritual life never dies, even if it is choked with uncertainty and pain. The search for God or the meaning of life these days is apparent in the development of the newer religions and in New Age utopian ways of thinking. Young people are looking for authentic witnesses of true values, and parents are seeking the best for their children.

As in the past, there are shadows and light: it will be the same tomorrow. Today as before, an anguished world seeks a Savior.

Today, we need the intervention of our God to deliver us from our sins, be they personal or communal, and to help us overcome our weaknesses and failings.

WHY IS LIFE SO HARD?

Why is life so hard? So many of my loved ones are dead. I am completely devastated and I can't function properly. Alcohol is a constant temptation as a way to escape, but thank goodness I have 'Alcoholics Anonymous'. Then I was robbed by someone I trusted! It's been like a nightmare. Happily I have children whom I adore. But I have become so negative about life. Do I have to endure all these trials and tribulations because God loves me? I would love to have an answer if there is one. I feel as though I am going through hell on earth.

* * *

May the few lines I write here be a comfort to you! No one can give you the precise answer, because the reason for our illnesses, bereavements, financial difficulties or betrayals by friends remains a mystery.

There has been much suffering in your life, and I sympathize with you sincerely. Why so many trials? I don't know. What I do know is that the Lord came to deliver us, that he has opened the gates of heaven forever. He himself suffered so much. So did Mary who had to watch her only Son suffer and die. When things hurt too much for you, think of Jesus, think of Mary. My answer is more silence than words. My answer is faith. I trust in God who knows all about suffering as we do. I trust in his promise of happiness. I believe in what he says: "Happy you who weep now: you shall laugh" (Lk 6: 21).

We can read about what happened to Job in the Old Testament. He was very rich and then suddenly he was deprived of everything. In a dramatic way he lost his entire family. He suffered a very painful illness. His friends tried to explain the reasons for his misfortunes. But they were wrong! They did not have the correct answer as to why his life became so miserable. Neither do I.

The story of Job, instead of providing an answer, invites us to place our trust in God.

Do the same in your prayers, and as well, take joy in your children. Embrace everything that brings sunshine into your life: your family, the help of your friends in AA, etc. Help suffering people. Smile on them and encourage them; be a witness of your faith in God. In doing these things, you will accomplish a lot and you will find the answers to your questions.

IS IT REALLY FAIR TO BRING CHILDREN INTO TODAY'S WORLD?

* * *

Society is blasé about life; it can be cold and cruel; it promotes values that are so often not Christian values.

Increasingly, life is hard and heartless. Men and women struggle in vain to find work and eke out a living, constantly worrying about a future over which they have no control. Life-altering decisions with stifling restrictions are often made by powerful financial institutions, governments and multinationals. Unexpected illness drains much needed strength and financial resources. And, on top of everything else, love is always under attack, hearts are broken and spirits are crushed.

What will become of those whom we love the most, our children? What will their tomorrows be like when we are no longer there to take care of them? Will they be strong enough to fly on their own? Will they have developed a thick enough skin so as not to suffer any fatal blows?

Even in school our children cannot be sheltered from bad things. Our parental influence is often ineffective, in religious matters, in sexual matters, in the transmission of true values and morals. Harmful influences replace our own, rendering us impotent. Our children are often the victims of unscrupulous 'pushers'. They become a statistic. Deprived of affection, bullied in a life without meaning, too many of them consider ending their own lives.

Or else, they look for distractions in drugs, alcohol, sex, things that yield immediate gratification. They are filled with disillusion and bitterness. Is their life worth living?

You ask: "Is it really fair or worthwhile to bring children into such a world? How can we adequately provide for their needs and their education? How can we as parents oversee their moral and spiritual formation? Isn't it wishful thinking to try to accomplish this and to work toward it?".

Here is my answer...

In spite of the clouds that accumulate and overshadow the future of our youth, we must believe in the sun, in the light that shines at the end of the tunnel.

A child is the greatest gift of God. A child is incomparable richness, the joy of the home, the hope for tomorrow, a living bud of great potential.

For those who believe in God, a child about to be born or newly born, even a child who is sick or disabled, receives divine life through baptism. This divine life is stronger than the forces of evil and will last forever.

A child is not only created for life on earth, with all its accompanying joy and sorrow, but also for life ever after, in the happiness of God, in such happiness that "no eye has seen and no ear has heard, things beyond the mind of man" (1 Co 2: 9).

It is indeed worth the effort to bring children into this world and to cooperate with the sublime work of creation. A child is always the greatest gift in a marriage. May parents love their children and assume their responsibility to form their lives and their values! May parents show their children the right path, the path to

God, the path of true life! May all parents put their hope in God who loves them, saves them, and protects their children!

Faith believes in a happy future for our children despite all opposition.

Yes, it is worthwhile to create children, to bring them into the world, as long as parents and educators who teach them believe that God lives within their souls.

Life is stronger than death. The forces of good overcome the forces of evil. Christ has saved the world. He has saved us as well. As Saint John wrote: "Anyone who has been begotten by God has already overcome the world" (1 Jn 5: 4). "Why are you so frightened, you men of little faith?" (Mt 8: 26).

Let us sow; let us scatter great handfuls of faith in the souls of our children. Despair occurs when nothing has been sown... The Divine Gardener, our Lord God, will see these seeds grow one day. Trust in him! He loves our children more than we do!

- IV -

THE CHURCH

The Fathers of the Church
Slavery
The Holocaust
Forgiveness
Secularization

ARE THERE TWO RELIGIONS: ONE FROM GOD AND ONE CREATED BY MEN?

When I was young, I received all my teaching from the Roman Catholic Church. The catechism taught me that all men had to belong to the Catholic Church in order to be saved.

I loved God and Jesus, but we were not encouraged to talk to them directly. I thought that my religion was the right one. We recited the rosary every night. Then, at the age of 27, I was given a Bible. I marveled as I read God's words and promises, and was shocked that they were never told to me.

Nothing is said in the Bible about the Church. Jesus teaches me to pray: "When you pray, enter your room and pray to your Father".

God was love and I was afraid of death. I never talked to Jesus to ask for his forgiveness and to be saved.

It seems to me that there are two religions: one from God and one that was developed by men.

* * *

I had to summarize a long letter to discuss the most important points. I have answered similar questions in my previous writings.

I refer my correspondent to the *Catechism of the Catholic Church*, published in 1992. It contains the complete teaching of the Church, a teaching drawn from the Word of God: the Bible and the Tradition inspired by the Holy Spirit.

I can't impose my faith on those who hold to a different doctrine. I pray that, in mutual respect, we remain faithful to the Spirit received from Jesus.

Contrary to the opinion of the questioner, the Bible often speaks of the Church. The Catholic Church goes back to Jesus' time. She is of apostolic origin and many biblical texts show the importance Jesus, her Founder, attached to her. He laid down his life for her (Ep 5: 25). We know that the Church is Christ's Body and that he is the Head of the Church (Col 1: 18). He has founded the Church on Peter and the Twelve Apostles (Mt 16: 18). He commissioned them to go forth and preach the Good News to all nations (Mt 28: 19). We are baptized in order to form one Body (I Co 12: 13). We are brothers and sisters, children of the same Father, not to live each in his or her own corner, but together, like a family, in Church.

Let's never separate Christ from his Body, the Church. Even if we do not belong to the Body of the Church because we fail to understand its importance, God will see our deep desire to please him. But, within the Church we find all the graces the Lord has given us: his integral and authentic teaching, pastors he has commissioned, sacraments of life, especially the Eucharist, the motherly presence of Mary, etc.

We can't take only certain passages in the Gospel and forget about the rest, neglecting the context and other words from the Lord. The excerpt quoted in the question in regard to prayer is one of many passages concerning prayer and doesn't include all the example and teaching received from Jesus. In the quote, the sacred writer underlines the importance of humility in prayer. But remember, Jesus, our Model, prayed by himself, but also with his disciples; he went to the temple and to the synagogue, "as he usually did" (Lk 4: 16).

Now that we are adults, we must try to better understand what we learned in religion when we were young. Exactly as we do in regard to secular sciences. For many Christians, their faith is still at the 'spoon-feeding' stage, whereas they have grown older and are more than able to feed themselves... We should imitate other Christians who nourish their faith through deepening their knowledge of Jesus, of the Church and of divine gifts; they become exemplary Christians and devoted Catholics; they sanctify themselves, in spite of human frailties.

As they grow older, certain people suddenly understand the value and riches of faith, but some do so outside the Catholic Church. This is not proof that the Church's doctrine is false; but it is still insufficiently understood.

I believe in Jesus. I also believe in the one, holy, Catholic and apostolic Church. I unite my profession of faith to that of millions and millions of Catholics, those of the past and those of today. I unite my profession of faith to that of all martyrs, mystics, missionaries, consecrated souls, and devoted laypeople of yesterday and today. Throughout the centuries and today, moved by the Holy Spirit, they have lived or still live a holy life as members of the Catholic Church.

WHO ARE THE 'FATHERS OF THE CHURCH'?

* * *

The title of 'Apostolic Fathers' was given by the Church to men who lived near the end of the first and the beginning of the second century, who recorded faithful versions of apostolic teaching (Dom Charles Poulet). Among their writings were The Didache, The Pastor of Hermas, the letter of Pope Clement, and the epistles of the martyr Saint Ignatius of Antioch.

There was also a group of writers called the 'apologists' in the second century and after. These Christian writers wrote to defend Christianity which was being persecuted for various reasons. They wrote to defend their faith and destroy prejudice. Among them we find renowed authors: Saint Justin and Saint Irenaeus, etc.

After the time of persecution, in the 4th century, there was the beginning of monasticism. At the same time, the Church went through many years of strong controversy in doctrinal matters, that of irremissible sins, baptism by heretics, etc. There were also heated debates concerning the Trinity and Christology. We must also mention heresies such as Donatism, Arianism, Nestorianism, Monophysitism and Pelagianism. Our Lord, in his Providence, sustained the great saints, inspired theologians and courageous pastors to steer the Church on the right course, in spite of hidden reefs and shallow waters. Many of them, shining with holiness, wrote immortal works and we call these people 'Fathers of the Church'.

Most of them lived between the second and eighth centuries; the fourth and fifth centuries were considered to be the golden age for this 'Patristic Period'. We can confidently add some names from later centuries, for example Saint Bernard in the twelfth century. These writers, from the earliest beginning of the Church who were inspired by the Word of God and proclaimed it, are our *'Fathers'* in faith.

There are a few names worth mentioning: in the East, Saints Cyprian, Athanasius, Ephrem, Gregory of Nazianzus, Gregory of Nyssa, Cyril, John Chrysostom, and, in the West, prestigious names such as Hilary, Ambrose, Jerome, Augustine and Gregory the Great. The list is long and far from complete here.

Let us admire the action of Providence in all ages, even today.

DID THE CHURCH APPROVE SLAVERY?

We know all that is written in the Bible about Ham, the ancestor of the Canaanites (Gn 9, 18 ss); slavery is indeed mentioned. The Bible that serves as a sort of library for the Christian religion is the basis of black slavery.

The blood letting of Africa was done in connivance with the Catholic Church... The Catholic Church did not raise its voice in opposition... For example, in the Antilles, the Catholic Church had slaves on her land.

Did those slaves have the respect and dignity of human beings?

* * *

The biblical passage you cite relates a primitive story used to explain the situation in Palestine where the Canaanites were dominated peaceably by the Semites and the Japhetites. It would be simplistic to see in this the basis for Black slavery.

We cannot judge the past by present standards. The Church could not change civil laws, like those in the Roman Empire where it was founded, or those that came later from colonized countries. She had to penetrate them with the Gospel. This is what she tried to do ever since the time of Saint Paul who proclaimed that we are all children of God, that there are no longer any slaves nor free men (Ga 3: 28).

Did some Christians sin in connivance? In too many cases, I believe this to be true. Good intention does not justify everything.

Pope John Paul II, profoundly moved, declared in Goree, Senegal, in 1992: "Men, women and children of the Black African continent have been victims of a disgraceful commerce in which the baptized have taken part, baptized who have not practiced their faith... We admit that this horrible sin of man against man, this sin of man against God, must, humbly and in all truthfulness, be confessed... We implore God's forgiveness".

In 1998, the Bishops of the Martinique, Guadeloupe, Cayenne and the Reunion offered a common declaration of which a summary is presented here:

"We share a large part of our origins with the African people. We will commemorate the 150th anniversary of the liberation of the slaves... We do not want to enclose ourselves in the walls of history. Christ remains our future.

In speaking of slavery, far be it from our intention to state a case, to denounce, or to justify it. Slavery, old as the world, continues to be rampant in our day. The better part of the powers in place formed a league for the systematic exploitation of certain people by other people. This was a grave collective sin. The Church was implicated in the system and participated in the ambiguities of History. Are we not in solidarity?

There were some priests, religious men and women who worked doggedly and heroically against the evil. So many missionaries contributed to the humanization and evangelization of these desperate situations".

Instead of limiting ourselves to a negative view, let us remember that we cultivate good fruits from the Gospel proclaimed by the members of the Church in less than ideal conditions. These good fruits can be seen in the world of teaching, hospitals and in the service of the poor, etc.

To each and everyone of us is the task of fighting against slavery, which is the domination of the strong over the weak, of man over woman, of employer over employee, the grip of money and power... Brotherly love must prevail.

Slavery, today, takes the name of drugs, prostitution, abuse of high finance, abuse of the media... There is genocide, in addition to uprooted people: Palestinians, Africans, Asians, Aboriginals...

Slavery is an action, but it can also be an omission...

"Serve one another", says Saint Paul (Ga 5: 13).

WHY HAS THE CATHOLIC CHURCH CLOSED HER EYES AGAINST THE MASSACRE?

Why has the Catholic Church closed her eyes on the massacre of so many millions of people in order to preserve her social position and wealth?

* * *

This is a brutal accusation. Such blanket condemnation calls for closer examination. I am not saying it is completely false, but are not we all members of the Church? It is easy to condemn the Church, that is to say others, the hierarchy especially, and to close our eyes to our own sins. We ourselves 'destroy' our brothers and sisters by our judgments, our false witness and our slanderous words.

The Catholic Church has spoken out and continues to rise up against numerous horrible injustices, against the massacre and the unjust sufferings of millions of people in many countries. We only have to read the many documents from the Pope and from our bishops. However, do we really read them? The Church strongly protests against contemporary genocides. Bishops, numerous priests, religious brothers and sisters and the Catholic laity die in the defense of human rights, for freedom of conscience, for human dignity. They cry out against violence. Martyrs die in defense of the voiceless, in China, in Algeria, Sudan, Pakistan, Mexico, Columbia... Are they not the Catholic Church?

That said, I do agree that the Church has not been as strong as it should have been during episodes of senseless killings in the past, be it in the time of the Holocaust or in other eras. The Pope does not hesitate to seek forgiveness. Remember his examination of conscience on the threshold of the new millennium: that the memory of so many mistakes and silence may be purified. He recalls the religious wars, bloody oppression, the Holocaust. The members of the Church were not totally to blame for these crimes; they were not always the most responsible, however they shared the guilt, most often by not voicing their disapproval of the atrocities.

In the *Declaration of Repentance* of the Church of France, September 30th 1997, Drancy, the French Bishops recalled the French Catholic Church's attitude under the Vichy regime, in the face of persecution of the Jews and the general anti-Semitism. Some bishops assented, by their silence, to the violations of human rights, although we cannot judge their conscience. Other courageous bishops protested, and steps were taken to save lives. Some priests, religious and laity performed heroic acts to save some Jewish people. Overall, however, indifference reigned. "This silence was a mistake. This weakness of the French Church and its historic responsibility toward the Jewish people are part of its history. We confess this mistake. We implore the pardon of God"(1.c.).

History moves on. Are you and I any better than those who lived before us? What is our own attitude in regard to people around us and to ongoing injustices happening in many countries?

WHAT WAS THE ROLE OF THE CHURCH IN THE HOLOCAUST?

* * *

Pope Pius XII was vehemently attacked on the subject of the Holocaust, of the Shoah. He was accused of keeping silent for fear of reprisals, as six million Jewish people were herded into concentration camps, dying of hunger and misery, or killed in gas chambers.

In March of 1998, a document, *We Remember. A Reflection on the Shoah*, issued by the Vatican, expressed the regrets of the Catholic Church for this genocide, the largest in history. It was received with mixed reviews. Some criticized the document for distinguishing between the Church itself and individual members. Members are blamed, not the doctrine, the sermons and the liturgy, with their anti-Semitic traditions. Others have pointed out that nothing really is said on the subject of Pius XII. Some would have preferred an explicit plea for pardon on the part of the Church (*The Tablet*).

Was it possible to add statements against Pius XII? Historic studies are only beginning. History is much more subtle than legends. Even when the Vatican releases all the documents pertaining to the reaction of the Church to the Shoah, the argument will without doubt continue, with some for, some against.

New York Rabbi David Dalin has proposed that Pope Pius XII be proclaimed "Righteous among the nations", the highest award given by the state of Israel to persons who were outstanding in assisting persecuted Jews during World War II. No other Pope has been so widely praised by Jews. Their gratitude testifies that he was genuinely and profoundly a righteous gentile (*Church World*, March 1, 2001, p. 11).

If Pius XII was silent, it was to keep from provoking an even greater evil. We know for a fact that Pius XII helped save many Jewish people, opening to them, at the risk of his own life, the territory of the Vatican, that many Jewish people, at the end of the war, expressed their gratitude to him.

The Vatican document, "*We remember...*", marks a large step forward in condemning anti-Semitism. Love, the central theme of the Gospel, has too often been neglected in the course of history. And history, our own history, has a tendency to repeat itself.

WHY IS THE CHURCH ASKING FORGIVENESS?

* * *

The Holy Spirit always breathes new life into the Church of Jesus Christ. We may understand her recent move: a request for forgiveness.

In the same manner, governments ask pardon for past mistakes against the First Nations, the Blacks, the respect of women. Take, for example, the attitude of the Prime Minister of Britain who asks for forgiveness for the suffering endured by the Irish during the great famine of the 19th Century. Let us listen to the apologies given by the white government of South Africa in regards to the apartheid, etc. We must not 'anesthetize' the memories. It would be damaging to the present generation, approving subconsciously the errors and the mistakes of the past. We are, in some way, co-responsible for our heritage.

John Paul II wanted the Church to make an examination of conscience for the new millennium. He wanted the Church to recognize her historical faults and ask pardon for the participation of some of her members in the tragedies of history: the Inquisitions, the schisms, the religious wars, the crusades, the slavery, the sufferings of the Indians, the Jews, women; and even in regard to individuals such as Galileo.

On September 10th, 1984, the Pope addressed himself to the native people at Saint Anne de Beaupre: "Your encounter with the Gospel not only has enriched you, but has enriched the Church. We know well that this has not been without difficulty, and sometimes not even without clumsiness".

The same Pope said in the Czech Republic, May 1995, in speaking of the religious wars: "Today, I, the Pope of the Church of Rome, in the name of all Catholics, ask pardon for all the wrongs that have been inflicted upon non-Catholics in the course of their turbulent history". Although both sides can share some blame, the Catholic Church recognizes the errors of certain of her members.

Such an attitude does not please all members of the Church. Some fear a negative image of the Church that will be the amusement of the atheists; the numerous fruits of sanctity throughout history seem to be forgotten.

Aware of the facts of history and without forgetting the socio-cultural context of the time, the Pope's actions open doors to ecumenism and help the members of the Church to renounce wrong-doings, to better live the Gospel and to do works of evangelization.

All humans sin against love. Christian men and women occasionally deviate from the Gospel. They do not always reflect the face of God. All the same, let us not forget the mass of martyrs and those millions of Christian men and women who have suffered and continue to suffer every day while protesting against injustice in our world.

CAN WE BLAME THEM IF SOME CHRISTIANS ARE RESENTFUL OF THE CATHOLIC CHURCH?

Can we blame them if some Christians are resentful of the Catholic Church? I am thinking in particular of those people of older generations who experienced an autocratic Church that seemed to preach little about the love of God but a great deal about sin and hell.

* * *

From today's viewpoint, the Church of yesteryear may appear to have been very severe, perhaps too much so! Sermons rigorously denounced sin, especially sexual sin, and words about hell and damnation echoed from the pulpit. Many were traumatized by these memories. But we must not conclude that the Good News of God's love was not shared as well. Fear could overshadow love, but love sanctified many. In fact, the love of God was not excluded from the sermons of earlier generations. Remember the devotions to the Sacred Heart, to the Blessed Sacrament, to the Passion of Christ and to the Virgin Mary. Fear was often used to motivate Christians to stay on the right road towards conversion, and then love took over to strengthen and maintain that conversion in faithfulness to good works and prayers.

Since Vatican II in the 1960's, the skies have cleared. There is no longer 'thunder and lightning' in today's preaching. Homilies now emphasize the love and mercy of a redeeming God. In this, I rejoice along with you! We can never hear enough about the immensity of God's tenderness towards us. This is the gospel message. This is the 'Good News' to soothe our broken spirits.

We must be on guard, nevertheless, to avoid taking God's love for granted or rendering it infantile and overly sentimental in order to excuse the choices we make as human beings.

Between the fear of sin and hell, and totally allowing our human nature to rule our actions, there is opportunity to show our love for God by keeping his commandments (Jn 14:15). Quietism, passiveness and inactivity are not the alternative to the austere practices and moral rigorism of Jansenism. These two extremes should be avoided so that the true love of our Lord can triumph, that perfect love that yields so much trust and joy.

HOW CAN WE COUNTER THE SECULARIZATION OF THE CHURCH?

In a secular world, we find ourselves as members of a Church which is secularizing before our very eyes. How can we counter the movement towards the secularization of the hierarchy and the People of God?

* * *

To what point is our Church being secularized, as a hierarchy or as the assembled People of God?

We can make some easy assertions but they are not always statements tinged with reality.

Evidently, today, as in the past, the Church is subjected to the influence of society and risks getting a bit bogged down with materialism or secularism, becoming less spiritual and a bit more profane. The Church, the Kingdom of Heaven begun on earth, is the yeast in the dough (Mt 13: 33). Its mission is not to be the yeast kept away from the dough, the heavy dough of humanity. It must remain the leaven of humanity.

We are the Church. It is for each one of us to spiritualize and not to secularize, in the bad sense of the meaning.

If the danger of the secularization of the Church exists – for the Church is not only spiritual – , there are signs in evidence that the Church is not ceasing to be divine. Divine in her origins, in her constitution, in the presence in her of Jesus and the Holy Spirit, in her revealed doctrines, in her sacraments which sanctify. Our priests follow in the footsteps of the saints; in spite of the difficulties, they guide us towards God. The laity, members of the Church, produce the fruits of astonishing holiness and are committed generously in the service of their brothers and sisters, especially the destitute. Let us see the good works of our holy Church, beyond her obvious weaknesses.

"See, I am doing a new thing! Now it springs up; do you not perceive it?" (Is 43: 19).

- V -

THE CHURCH (continued)

WHY IS THE CHURCH SO SLOW TO EVOLVE?

* * *

Some people are impatient with the apparent slow progress of the Church. The evolution of the Church seems stalled by the inertia of her leaders. In a world which moves increasingly fast, the Church seems reactionary or even regressive.

Others believe the opposite... The Church, since Vatican II, was transformed, they proclaim; the Church isn't the same and it betrays the past.

Who is right? Spiritual adolescents or spiritual older people?

The Pope is often the target of extremists from both sides.

Taken to the extreme, both tendencies are excessive and dangerous. They become a liberalism which betrays or a conservatism which suffocates.

Moved by the Holy Spirit, under the guidance of her pastors, the Church advances wisely, step-by-step; but she is advancing. The Church is not a mummy, nor a piece of antiquity; she is the living Body of the living Christ.

Let us have confidence in her and let us have confidence in our pastors.

WHY DOESN'T THE CHURCH FOLLOW
THE SAME LAWS IN EVERY COUNTRY?

Besides Sundays, are there other feastdays of obligation in the liturgical calendar?

Why doesn't the Catholic Church follow the same laws and the same customs in all countries of the world? For example: the days of obligation are not the same everywhere.

* * *

The things that are essential are accepted by Catholics everywhere, today as in the past: we share an identical faith in the Lord, we express the same love for God and neighbor, we believe in the same doctrine and we accept the same sacraments... Sunday is celebrated by Christians all over the world; it is the Lord's Day.

There are disciplinary rules of lesser importance which may differ from country to country, from diocese to diocese, just as there are differences in the daily conduct of families which profess the same faith and adhere to the same human values.

Holy days of obligation may vary from country to country. We all celebrate the same Christian feastdays but for various reasons they may be designated as days of obligation in some countries and not in others.

The *Code of Canon Law* (Can. 1246) provides a list of feastdays of obligation: the Lord's Day is always the primary holy day of obligation, the Nativity of Our Lord Jesus Christ, the Epiphany, the Ascension of Christ, the feast of the Body and Blood of Christ, the feast of the Mother of God, her Immaculate Conception, her Assumption, the feast of Saint Joseph, the feast of the Apostles Saints Peter and Paul, and the feast of All Saints. In each country, the episcopate, with the approval of the Holy See, may suppress certain feasts of obligation or transfer them to the following Sundays.

According to Canon 1246, the Canadian Conference of Catholic Bishops (CCCB) decreed that the feastdays of obligation in Canada are: all Sundays, Christmas and the feast of Mary the Mother of God (January 1st). It transferred the feasts of the Epiphany, the Ascension, and the Body and Blood of Christ (the Blessed Sacrament) to the Sunday following the actual day.

In the United States, the feastdays of obligation are: all Sundays, the Immaculate Conception, Christmas, the feast of Mary the Mother of God (January 1st), Ascension Thursday (in some dioceses, it's transferred to the following Sunday), the Assumption of Mary, the feast of All Saints.

Our Christian life is to love God and our neighbor. With the help of the Holy Spirit, we strive to imitate Jesus, and, with our legitimate differences, we continue our journey towards our Father's House.

HOW IS A POPE ELECTED?

* * *

The choice of a Pope has not always been what it is today.

The Pope is the bishop of Rome, the successor of Saint Peter to whom the Lord Jesus has entrusted the Church (Mt 16: 18). During the course of centuries, he was often chosen in the same way as were chosen the other bishops of the Church, that is, by the local clergy and the faithful. Too often, however, during the Middle Ages, the emperor chose the bishop of Rome. At the time of the Iron Age, towards the end of the Middle Ages, the bishop of Rome was even chosen by the great Roman families who were anxious to find favor with the new Pope. During that time, the night of the Middle Ages, some Popes were murdered. The bishopric of Rome was all the more coveted because, since the time of the Carolingians in the 8th century, the Pontifical States were attached to the Roman See.

For a while, there was an unfortunate lay investiture: the powerful suzerain, emperor or king, would confer on the Pope the emblems of his authority. Of course, a lay leader could never confer the spiritual power on the Pope or on the bishops. All bishops, the Pope included, receive their spiritual authority through the laying on of hands by other bishops, successors of the apostles. Their spiritual authority came from and continues to come from apostolic tradition.

In 1059, Pope Nicolas II decreed that, from then on, only the cardinals could elect the Pope. In this way, religious freedom was preserved in the choice of a Pope. Thus the selection of Popes was improved and the danger of simony (the purchase of ecclesiastic preferments) disappeared.

Nowadays, within a few days after the death of a Pope, all cardinals meet at the Vatican and, in a conclave (that is, in a locked room, *con clave*, under key), secretly and without undue influence, they elect the man who will be the next bishop of Rome, the Pope, the supreme leader of the Catholic Church, the pastor to whom Christ has given the power to bind or loose, and to strengthen his brothers (Mt 16: 18-19; Lk 22: 32).

WILL THE POPE BE THE LAST POPE?

I have read many books that say that this latest Pope is really the last Pope. What do you think?

* * *

There are many prophecies on the Popes, for example those that have been falsely attributed to Saint Malachy. Are they always true? I doubt it.

In order to predict that this Pope will be the last Pope, or that there will only be two or three more after him, we have to be able to predict the end of the world, the date of the end of time. Unfortunately we don't know this. My answer may disappoint those who believe the 'doomsday' prophets; it is the answer upheld by the teachings of the Church and the Pope.

In the 19th century, it was said that Pope Pius IX would be the last Pope; it has been said for others as well. There is indeed nothing new under the sun.

John Paul II confirmed that we do not know the exact moment when the history of humanity will be over. The reality, he says, is that the end has already begun. Christ did not reveal when it would be over. Why then should we seek to know? Isn't it better to remain always ready and live our Christian lives to the fullest while we wait? We should prepare for our own personal end, be ready for our own death.

Certainly we can wonder about the succession of the popes. Who will be the last? We don't know.

ON WHAT BASIS DOES THE CHURCH CHOOSE A DATE FOR EASTER?

I would like to know the reason why the Catholic Church chooses different dates for Easter. I have often wondered why.

* * *

Both Jews and Christians celebrate Easter, but the feast doesn't have the same meaning for all. The Jewish celebration of Easter, *Pessah*, is a commemoration of the passage from slavery into liberty, from Egypt to the Promised Land, under Moses' leadership. At Yahweh's request, religious ceremonies are held to mark this unique event. A pascal meal, *Seder*, inaugurates the celebration.

Easter reminds Christians of another passage: Christ's victory over death and sin, through his passion and resurrection, and our own final passage from death to eternal life. We unite ourselves to Christ's passage, in Baptism and the Eucharist. Sunday is a memorial of Easter, as we celebrate Christ's death and resurrection.

Easter is the first Christian holiday the early Church solemnized, along with Pentecost. Christians prepare themselves for Easter during Lent.

At the beginning of the Church, the date for Easter was not the same everywhere. There were attempts to find an agreement. A long dispute followed. The astronomical calculation of the date differed from region to region. Finally a solution was reached: the feast of Easter would always be on a Sunday. The Council of Nicaea, in 325, proclaimed that Easter Sunday would always be the first Sunday after the full spring moon. As a result, Easter Sunday can never occur before March 22nd or after April 25th.

The date of Easter is the same for Catholics and Protestants; not so with the majority of Oriental Churches (they make use of a different calendar). Representatives of most Christian Churches met these past years in an effort to agree on the same date.

We must celebrate Easter with hope and joy. We should unite ourselves to the Lord's resurrection, 'making our Easter duty', as we used to say, with a purified heart, welcoming our Saviour's love, uniting ourselves to him in the Eucharist. This is why the Church has enacted the following law:

"Once admitted to the blessed Eucharist, each of the faithful is obliged to receive holy communion at least once a year. This precept must be fulfilled during paschal time, unless for a good reason it is fulfilled at another time during the year" (*Code of Canon Law*, Can. 920).

CAN YOU ANSWER ME WITH A YES OR NO?

Please answer yes or no.

A number of years ago, the Church gave permission to eat meat on Friday; afterwards, the bishops asked us to practice abstinence on Friday, as of old.

Is it a sin if I eat meat on Friday? Yes or no?

Is it a sin if I eat meat on Ash Wednesday? Yes or no?

Is it a sin if I eat meat on Good Friday? Yes or no?

* * *

The Church would like us to behave as adults. She hopes that we will grow in our faith, that we will understand why we have to act in certain ways. With an enlightened conscience, we would find the necessary answers and grow in our fidelity to the Lord's commandments.

There are precepts of the Church we must normally obey in conscience. But what about our health, the requirements of our position in life, etc.? Circumstances may arise that may influence our best intentions. This is why it may sometimes be difficult to answer with a simple yes or no.

The Church's precepts are given us to help us observe the Lord's laws. One of the Lord's commandments is to do penance, each according to his or her possibilities (*Code of Canon Law*, Can. 1249-1253). Accordingly, the Church invites her faithful to do penance, especially at certain times of the year, through fasting and abstinence.

"Abstinence from meat, or from some other food, as determined by the Episcopal Conference, is to be observed on all Fridays, unless a solemnity should fall on a Friday. Abstinence and fasting are to be observed on Ash Wednesday and Good Friday" (*Code of Canon Law*, Can. 1251).

The Catholic bishops of Canada, as well as the Catholic bishops of the United States, decreed that the days of fast and abstinence would be Ash Wednesday and Good Friday. Fridays are days of abstinence, but, in Canada, Catholics may, on Friday, replace abstinence with works of charity and pious exercises (April 14, 1985).

The law of abstinence is an obligation for all faithful over the age of fourteen. As for fasting, it is an obligation for all faithful who have reached their maturity and before they turn 60.

Penance is well signified by fast, prayer and alms (*The Catechism of the Catholic Church*, Nos 1430, 1434), but the Church primarily stresses interior disposition, the love of God and neighbor. She recommends prayer and charity, a sincere conversion and an interior repentance. Nobody should boast about fast and abstinence, not to be a hypocrite (Mt 6: 16).

Voluntary negligence with regard to the Church's laws on penance is not exempt from sin, since it reveals a lack of vigilance in following the teachings of Christ: "Therefore, you too must stand ready because the Son of Man is coming at an hour you do not expect" (Mt 24: 44).

WHY HAS THE CHURCH PUBLISHED A CATECHISM?

* * *

Many Christians seek a clear affirmation of the content of their faith. This catechism testifies to the faith of the Church.

The new catechism is one of the 'good fruits' that originated from Vatican II. It is a collegial work, thanks to the efforts of extensive consultation among bishops, numerous theologians, catechists and experts the world over.

Publication of this catechism signifies an important stage in the life of the modern Church. It renders a precious service to the pastors and catechists of today.

It is certainly not the only religious document to be published in recent years. Sixteen documents originated from Vatican II. In addition, there are numerous encyclicals and pontifical letters, multiple interventions of Roman Congregations, as well as messages from our bishops.

Nevertheless, the *Catechism of the Catholic Church* "is an event of great importance and historic significance" (John Paul II). The solemn date of promulgation of this catechism was December 7, 1992.

From the time of the Old Testament, teachings or *didache* attempted to transmit the Word of God to transform life. In the New Testament, the gospels, at first oral and then written, became the first catechism. At the end of the first century, in Syria, the *Didache*, or *Doctrine of the Apostles*, was written to instruct catechumens and others.

Around the Middle Ages, the writings of Saint Augustine, Alcuin, Peter Lombard, and of Saint Thomas Aquinas, to name but a few, are worth mentioning.

Catechisms or similar documents were not plentiful before the invention of the printing press. But, by the 16th century, catechisms were very much in evidence. At that time, the *Catechism of the*

Council of Trent, or the *Catechism of Saint Pius V*, or the *Roman Catechism*, was published. It was an extensive work, similar to today's *Catechism of the Catholic Church*.

At the same time, there were catechisms written by Saint Peter Canisius (around 1555), Martin Luther and John Calvin.

The catechisms of Saint Robert Bellarmin, Dupanloup, and Saint Pius X are also significant works.

The 1992 *Catechism of the Catholic Church* is inspired by the Holy Scriptures, the Tradition of the Church, the Magisterium, the Liturgy, the Fathers of the Church, etc. Its 600 pages are divided into four sections: the creed, the liturgy (mainly the sacraments), morality and prayer. Our Lord is always at its center. The catechism offers a synthesis of the doctrines of faith and the moral precepts of the gospels. To help with the comprehension, there is a Subject Index at the back of the book, as well as a Table of Contents.

The *Catechism of the Catholic Church* is not a manual of catechesis as such, rather it is an important instrument for catechesis. This catechism is the basis and the point of reference for local catechisms, national and diocesan, that are necessary to connect the different cultures, ages and contexts, and proposes the most appropriate methods. As John Paul II wrote on October 11, 1992: "This catechism is not intended to replace the local catechisms duly approved...".

Every Catholic who seeks to better understand his or her faith is advised to look through the *Catechism of the Catholic Church*. It will facilitate the efforts of the new evangelization.

This publication "is an important contribution to the work of renewal in all of our ecclesiastical life" (John Paul II).

WHAT IS THE CHURCH'S POSITION REGARDING BLESSINGS?

I am curious. I know of an elderly lady who asked her priest to bless some olive oil and some salt, and he complied.

When I asked her why she wanted this done, she answered: "When I put this salt in my salt shaker, all the food that it flavors will contain graces from God. And as for the oil, I use it for healing what ails me".

What is the Church's position regarding such blessings, or the blessing of medals, water, candles, etc? What special properties does such an action impart to inanimate objects?

* * *

There are many rituals of benediction, some of which are quite recent. The Church allows blessings of living beings and also inanimate objects. The *Catechism of the Catholic Church* discusses *sacramentals*, which include the blessings you question.

In our faith, we assume that sincere prayers will obtain grace and blessings from the Lord. Without prayer, such actions are empty of meaning and border on superstition.

We are not only spiritual beings. Our bodies with our physical senses need concrete signs and actions to sanctify our everyday life and activity.

There are seven *sacraments*, efficacious signs of grace instituted by Christ: Baptism, Confirmation, Eucharist, Penance, Anointing of the Sick, Holy Orders and Matrimony. They signify important stages in our earthly life, nurture our faith life, provide healing and direction. Within the seven, the Eucharist has a central place. It is the sacrament of all sacraments.

Sacramentals, however, are instituted by the Church, signifying effects which are obtained through the intercession and prayers of the Church. They help us to sanctify the many things around us that are useful to our daily living. They "always include a prayer, often accompanied by a specific sign, such as the laying on of hands, the sign of the cross, or the sprinkling of holy water" (*Catechism of the Catholic Church*, No 1668).

Sacramentals "prepare us to receive grace and dispose us to cooperate with it" (*Catechism of the Catholic Church*, No 1670). Among them are the blessings of persons, objects, meals, places, etc. Other sacramentals have lasting importance because they 'consecrate' persons to God, or reserve objects and places for liturgical use, for example a church or an altar.

When a blessing is given by a priest, representing Christ, it imparts a particular importance to the action. But lay people are also called to bless. For example, spouses may bless one another, parents may bless their children at bedtime, etc., and blessings can be given in solemn moments such as the beginning of the New Year, etc. (Can. 1168).

In addition to the sacraments instituted by Christ and the sacramentals instituted by the Church, a few words should be added here regarding other forms of religious practice, sometimes termed *para-sacramentals* because they are like sacramentals and are used in popular devotions, like the salt and olive oil blessed for this lady.

These days we hear more and more about the increase in popular devotions, with joyous assemblies of people, special events and celebrations. We must not look down upon this kind of piety, because there is great value in it. Even the popes have attested to the sense of God's presence, trust in him, sincere and spontaneous worship, and generosity of spirit within these devotions. It is true that we must be cautious not to slip into superstitious or excessively sentimental devotions. Popular devotions will always exist. They support our faith and are an extremely valuable resource for evangelization. They are a grace and a calling, says the Pope.

Therefore, as long as the focus is on the liturgy, a form of public worship, the Church approves of the veneration of relics, processions, and sacred objects such as statues, rosaries, medals, pictures, candles, palms, holy oil, holy water, etc., because all these things nourish our prayers and encourage a closer relationship with the Lord and the saints in heaven. They enrich Christian life.

SHOULD WE BELIEVE IN THE HOLY SHROUD OF TURIN?

Does the Shroud contain the true image of Jesus?

* * *

In May 1898, when the Holy Shroud was on display, a photographer, Segundo Pia, took pictures using a simple camera. As the plates were developed, he found out, to his utter surprise, that they were not a negative image of the Shroud, but the image of a man with light and shadow and the relief of a sculpted figure. He had obtained a positive image on his negative plate because the Holy Shroud is itself a negative. The sensational news spread rapidly and scientists tried to find the reason for the negative imprint of the Holy Shroud, an image which preceded the discovery of photography by many centuries.

Studies continue, more so since 1931, when Giuseppe Enrie produced excellent photos of the Shroud. Dr Pierre Barbet, from Paris, carefully studied the effects of the passion on the body represented on the cloth.

Father Edward Wuenschel, an American Redemptorist, dedicated his life to researching the Holy Shroud. After 1930, the increase in published work on the subject fascinated millions of readers. The historical, theological and biblical features of the Holy Shroud were the topic for many magazine articles and conferences.

Father Adam Ottorbein, another Redemptorist, succeeded Father Wuenschel in 1950. He founded the 'Holy Shroud Guild' to spread the knowledge of the Holy Shroud and to encourage further studies by learned scientists. It became clear that the Holy Shroud was not a painting.

In 1978, the Holy Shroud was exposed for veneration. A sophisticated technology was used for skillful studies. The chemicals and fibers in the Shroud were examined closely, using the most modern instruments and laboratory analyses. The results were highly publicized. In 1988, some experts concluded that the Holy Shroud was a forgery dating from the Middle Ages. However, few were aware that the particles of the Shroud used for the carbon-dating tests were all from the same piece, damaged in 1532 by fire and water. The cloth was contaminated.

Recently, positive results have been obtained. There is now botanical evidence obtained by pollen experts: on the Shroud, they found traces of plants which, in their combination, exist only in Palestine; the Shroud presents the likeness of a man having suffered the Roman crucifixion, according to details mentioned in the Gospel, etc.; there is resemblance between the Holy Shroud of Turin and the Sudarium of Orvieto, the cloth that would have been over Jesus' head in the tomb (Jn 20: 7).

In 1998, the Holy Shroud was again displayed for veneration in Turin. Millions of faithful went to contemplate it, including Pope John Paul II. Another veneration of the Shroud was made possible during Jubilee 2000.

Scientists from different continents, Europe, Asia, America and Australia still pursue their studies of the Holy Shroud of Turin. We find pictures of the Holy Shroud everywhere; the Shroud and its message continue to be the focus of annual conferences. Fathers Fred Brinkmann and John P. Kennington, American Redemptorists, still promote the Holy Shroud apostolate.

SHOULDN'T WE FEAR FOR THE FUTURE OF THE CHURCH?

I am afraid for the Church. She is experiencing dark times and everything seems to be getting worse. Don't you think so?

* * *

I will not proclaim that everything is going perfectly well. The image of the Church is often a caricature and a mockery. The media make a great to-do about sexual and physical abuse within the Church and yet keep silent about the sublime beauty of the Church, Body of Christ, and her constant spiritual achievements. Just as there were persecutions and heresies in the Roman empire and afterwards, the Church is still cruelly suffering in communist and totalitarian countries, and there are modern pressures on her from the New Age movement and so many heterogeneous beliefs.

The earthly paradise that baby boomers dreamed of after the war, was but an illusion. When they liberalized institutions and got rid of taboos, they destroyed important values and were unable to rebuild. The events of the 1960's in favor of sexual, social and religious freedom, led to confusion in a pluralistic society. These days, you have to surf a long time on the Internet to find traces of morality, true love and happiness. They have been replaced by sentimentality, individualism, materialism, extreme thrills and a 'live for the moment' philosophy.

However, not everything is somber. There are pessimistic people, short-sighted Christians, who forget about the constant blossoming of the Lord's actions. I remain confident and optimistic. Jesus said, before returning to his Father: "Be brave: I have conquered the world" (Jn 16: 33); "I will not leave you orphans" (Jn 14: 18). "Do not be afraid", says the Pope, "the new century will not be a century of darkness, but of God's love". Like Saint Augustine facing the Vandals, the Vicar of Christ is convinced that the gathering clouds of today do not signify the end of the world, but the beginning of a new society.

In a century from now, people will be full of admiration as they look back on the marvels of today. They will talk about extraordinary popes, they will be amazed at Christian youth festivals, they will remember our new movements and communities, they will make a long list of saints and martyrs, they will glorify God for Vatican II and the unexpected Church renewal.

They will admire the dream Pope John Paul II had when Christians entered into the new millennium: the Church will "sail to the deep sea and not only be in her port" (*Novo Millennio Ineunte*). The Church will fight poverty and social injustice. The Church will keep bringing the Good News to all people. She will reach out to all nations.

- VI -

THE SACRAMENTS

WHY SHOULD I HAVE MY CHILD BAPTIZED?

Why should I have my child baptized? Aren't all babies children of God?

* * *

This child whom you love so much is also loved by God. With his grace, you and your spouse have created this special youngster, this marvelous miracle of life that you now hold in your arms or who plays happily at your side. What is more beautiful than a sleeping child or that first smile? This gift from God is your child, to whom you would give the world, even your own life! Your love is so great!

Why should your child be baptized? Isn't he already a child of God? Yes, certainly, but...

We also have the teachings of Jesus; he is our God who came among us to redeem us. His words of salvation show us the road to the Kingdom, for you, for me, for your child. It is a road of unlimited happiness, a gateway to his family, the way to heaven! For the benefit of your dear child, take note of the words of Christ:

"Unless a man is born through water and the Spirit, he cannot enter the Kingdom of God" (Jn 3: 5); "He who believes and is baptized will be saved" (Mk 16: 16); "...and everyone of you must be baptized in the name of Jesus Christ..." (Ac 2: 38); "Go, therefore, make disciples of all the nations; baptizing them in the name of the Father and of the Son and of the Holy Spirit" (Mt 28: 19).

Jesus tells us how we may enter into his Kingdom: through baptism.

No doubt that God wants all human beings to be saved. The Lord in his mercy never refuses heaven to those who live good and decent lives and, who through no fault of theirs, are not aware of the necessity of baptism.

Can you deny your child this priceless grace? Since you love him so much, why would you wait to give him such a wonderful gift? Through baptism we experience the "cleansing water of rebirth" (Tt 3: 5).

Through baptism, we participate in the death and resurrection of Jesus (Col 2: 12). I am sure you want your child to share in Christ's glorious resurrection. Baptism gives new life that leads to eternal life. It is the supernatural life, the divine life within us. A life called to grow through the other sacraments such as Confirmation, to be nourished by the Eucharist, to be healed through the sacrament of Penance. It is a life that will blossom in heaven; it is eternal life offered by Jesus.

Through baptism we receive the Holy Spirit and become children of God. "And if we are children we are heirs as well: heirs of God and coheirs with Christ..." (Rm 8: 17).

It is true, in a general sense, that we can all call ourselves children of God. However, if we accept Jesus into our lives, we become God's children in a special way. "To all who accept him he gave power to become children of God" (Jn 1: 12). Through baptism, we welcome Jesus into our lives and we enter into a rich divine filiation; we become God's adopted children, co-inheritors with Christ. And also, baptism unites all of us, God's children, into a large and wonderful family, the Church: "For by one Spirit we were baptized into one body" (1 Co 12: 13). This same body is the Church, of which Christ is the head (Col 1: 18).

In baptism we experience a second birth, a new birth in which we enter the world of the risen Christ and the Trinity.

Why should you have your child baptized? For all of the above reasons. Through baptism, God's graces are activated, uniting your son or daughter with Jesus to share in his resurrection.

I PREFER TO WAIT... I AM ALLOWING MY CHILD TO DECIDE LATER WHETHER OR NOT HE WANTS TO BE BAPTIZED

* * *

Parents occasionally delay baptizing their children. They say that they respect the freedom of their children. It happens that they scarcely understand the effects of baptism. For parents and godparents, the preparation for baptism always turns out to be profitable and we must congratulate the sacramental initiation teams, those who prepare them for baptism. Priests and preparation teams meet with the parents with kindness and cordiality. They know that the parents want the best for their children. All of the community is invited to rejoice with them and all baptisms should be a family celebration, fervent and festive.

Grandparents wish that their grandchildren receive the blessing of divine life without delay. They are deeply saddened when the baptism is put off to a later date. They sometimes believe that they are responsible of a serious negligence. They should serenely discuss with the parents the suffering and the desire that they have. They are allowed to hope that one day the richness of baptism will be discovered. Then, baptized, the child, hopefully, will be raised as a Catholic so that baptism, a new birth, will have all the benefits. A young unbaptized person, having no concrete and sacramental bonds with the Church, risks even more of becoming prey of the sects.

The Pope reminds us of the necessity of baptism and the age-old custom of baptizing the children. Also, the *Code of Canon Law* stipulates: "Parents are obliged to see that their infants are baptized within the first few weeks. As soon as possible after the birth, indeed even before it, they are to approach the parish priest to ask for the sacrament for their child, and to be themselves duly prepared for it. If the infant is in danger of death, it is to be baptized without any delay" (Can. 867).

On October 20th 1980, the Congregation for the Doctrine of Faith published the *Instruction for the Baptism of Children*. This *Instruction*, approved by the Pope, reminds us of the practice of the Church, from apostolic times in the eastern and in the western worlds, that of baptizing children. It is sufficient to mention the teaching of saints of the first centuries: Irenaeus, Augustine, Hippolytus, Cyprian, etc.

The child, like all human beings, needs the salvation that only Jesus can bring. God calls him or her to become his child without delay. The gifts and spiritual dynamism placed in the subconscious of the very young will help and stimulate them as they grow up.

To baptize a child is not an invasion of his freedom, not any more than having him born or in educating him of true values. To be deprived of baptism is to be deprived of something essential. Baptism provides access to the true freedom. It deposits in the heart of the child the seeds of faith and life eternal (*Instruction*).

I HAVE TWO GRANDCHILDREN WHO ARE NOT BAPTIZED. WHAT CAN I DO?

I have two grandchildren who are not baptized. Their father refuses to allow it. One of them is sick and will soon die. I am sad and would like him to become God's child through baptism. What can I do? I am so unhappy.

* * *

Baptism, necessary for salvation, is the sign and the instrument of God who frees us from original sin and allows us participate fully in divine love.

Let's hope that the children's father will soon allow them to be baptized.

If a child is critically ill, you or somebody else does not need permission to baptize him. It is stated in the *Code of Canon Law*: "If the infant is in danger of death, it is to be baptized without any delay" (Can. 867, 2). "An infant of catholic parents, indeed even of non-catholic parents, may in danger of death be baptized even if the parents are opposed to it" (Can. 868, 2). The immediate baptism of a child is prescribed by the Church, since she doesn't know of other means to ensure children will enter into eternal bliss (*Pastoralis actio*, No 13).

"Baptism... is necessary for salvation, either by actual reception or at least by desire... It is validly conferred only by a washing in real water with the proper form of words" (Can. 849). You only have to pour water on the forehead while you say: "I baptize you in the name of the Father, and of the Son and of the Holy Spirit".

If you do baptize this child who is seriously ill, make sure you tell your parish priest of your actions.

As for your other grandchild who is in good health, you are bound to wait for the consent of the parents, of at least one of them, according to the Church's legislation: "For an infant to be baptized lawfully it is required: that the parents, or at least one of them, or the person who lawfully holds their place, give their consent; that there be a well-founded hope that the child will be brought up in the Catholic religion..." (Can. 868).

IS BEING CALLED CHILD OF GOD A PRIVILEGE RESERVED FOR THOSE WHO ARE BAPTIZED?

Is being called child of God a privilege reserved exclusively for those who are baptized or who believe in Christ? This is what is written in the Gospel of Saint John (1: 12).

If the non-baptized are not called children of God, what are they called?

* * *

We are all creatures of God. We depend on God. All humans are called to salvation; Christ died for all. We can say, in a way, we are all children of God.

The title of sons or daughters of God is often used in the Bible, in favor of people who have never been baptized. This title emphasizes their link with the Lord; especially with respect to the chosen people, the descendants of Israel.

However, we enter into a genuine filial relationship through baptism required by Jesus. The deep relationship established between God and us at baptism is a unique and beautiful reality! We truly become reborn, new creatures, children of God. We participate in his divine life, a life that will continue in eternity.

The *Catechism of the Catholic Church* affirms of each human being: "The dignity of the human person is rooted in his creation in the image and likeness of God... It is in Christ, Redeemer and Savior, that the divine image, disfigured in man by the first sin, has been restored to its original beauty and ennobled by the grace of God" (Nos 1700-1701).

"He who believes in Christ becomes a son of God. This filial adoption transforms him by giving him the ability to follow the example of Christ" (No 1709)

"Everyone moved by the Spirit is a son of God" (Rm 8: 14). The true divine filial relation comes to us from Christ. "To all who did accept him, he gave power to become children of God" (Jn 1: 12).

I DO NOT FEEL REMORSE FOR MY SINS. WILL I BE SAVED?

Sometimes I worry that I may not be saved. I have tried but have never felt remorse for my sins. I ask God for a contrite heart, but in vain. I implore you, minister of God, pray for me and for my conversion.

* * *

You are sorry that you are not sorry... Isn't this proof that you do feel remorse for your sins?

In your faith, you wish to please God, which includes contrition for your sins. You even pray to God about this matter. Your remorse is evident even though it is implied.

You reproach yourself. Because you regret your sins!

Don't associate the sincere remorse you feel for your sins with some emotion of repentance. Such emotion can accompany your remorse, but it is not necessary, especially in periods of spiritual dryness.

Repentance for your sins can also be accompanied – due to our poor human frailty – by an attraction to do further wrong.

True regret of one's sins develops through faith and the love of God. Such faith and love of God give us strength to avoid evil and dangerous situations, and to handle more or less voluntary temptations.

Be at peace! Let your love grow. In loving Jesus, you will increasingly regret in your heart anything that would distance you from that love, and that is what sin is.

Above all, you will be making progress, with your eyes fixed on him. Don't stop!

IS IT TRUE THAT SAINTS SIN SEVEN TIMES A DAY?

* * *

May I quote the Bible: "There is no virtuous man on earth who, doing good, is ever free of sin" (Qo 7: 20); "There is no man who does not sin" (I K 8: 46); "Both Jew and pagan sinned", wrote Saint Paul (Rm 3: 23); they are purified by Jesus Christ's redemptive grace. We may say to the Lord: "No one is virtuous by your standard" (Ps 143: 2). Jesus was like us, except that he was without sin (Heb 4: 15) and Mary, full of grace, was immaculate by the preventive action of Jesus, her Son, the Redeemer.

We are all weak and limited and not without imperfections, when we compare ourselves to God's holiness. "... The virtuous man falls seven times..." (Pr 24 : 16). If the just man sins seven times, that is frequently, then how often must we ourselves do so?

Those who claim they are without sin are often far away from God, from the brightness of his light. In their darkness or half-light, they can't see the dust that every day is settling on their souls, the dust of their more or less deliberate sins. The more the saints made progress on the road to holiness, the more they realized and confessed that they were sinners before God.

God, the Sun of our lives, helps us discover that we are sinners, focusing on ourselves, proud and careless in our love, prone to passions, sinful by omission as well as by our actions. "If we say we have no sin in us, we are deceiving ourselves and refusing to admit the truth" (I Jn 1: 8).

A Christian, who is anxious to please God, will never become withdrawn and will never be disheartened. He or she will not become scrupulous, but will focus his or her gaze on the Lord and will live joyfully as God's child.

Like the Little Flower, he or she will exclaim: "I rejoice for being imperfect...", not to make peace with spiritual weakness, but to humbly confess that holiness comes from God alone.

CAN WE CONFESS OUR SINS BY TELEPHONE?

* * *

Religious and cultural changes explain why confession over the telephone has at times been suggested. The problems created by the shortage of priests in our western countries prompts some of the faithful to dream of new solutions. This is why certain people favor confession by telephone, letter or e-mail.

Can technical developments threaten what is sacred?

Since the end of the 19th century, there is a fascinating controversy in regard to confession by telephone in case of emergency. I repeat: in case of emergency... According to the unanimous consent of theologians, there is no possibility of confession by telephone if there is no case of urgency. But, if a person or a community can't go to confession, while there is an imminent danger of death, can they receive the sacrament over the telephone? In 1884, the Sacred Penitentiary refused to take a position on the matter. The problem was considered a doctrinal problem, to be discussed among moralists. This response cast doubt on the validity in regard to confession by telephone in case of emergency. Some believed that there was a certain possibility of validity in case of absolute necessity; the majority were against it. As for its lawfulness, they knew it depended on the Church's authority.

Nothing was solved by the *Code of Canon Law* published in 1917. The 1983 *Code* states: "Except for a just reason, confessions are not to be heard elsewhere than in a confessional" (Can. 964, 3); some interpreted this rule as a negative reply regarding the use of the telephone.

Confession by correspondance had already been condemned in 1602 by Pope Clement VIII.

Those opposed to the validity of confession by telephone, even in case of emergency, cite the constant Tradition of the Church against such a procedure; the physical presence of the penitent before a confessor appears to be a necessity. Others, who believe in the validity of confession by telephone in case of emergency, say that the situation is new, caused by technological advances in sound transmission and that there is a moral presence in this method of communicating.

The primary problem is the necessary physical presence of the penitent and the confessor, the union of matter and form.

The American Secretariat for the Liturgy reminds us that no sacrament may be received by electronic device. All liturgical celebrations require the physical presence of the faithful and the physical presence of the bishop, priest, deacon or presiding minister. For the sacrament of reconciliation in particular, only the physical presence of the priest near the penitent may be a sign of the meeting with the Father who welcomes and forgives the sinner. The Secretariat declares that electronic communication by telephone, television, video or internet is not sufficient for the celebration of the sacraments. It seems to me that this is the official position of the Church.

Confession by telephone is forbidden under all normal circumstances. I believe that Rome never published a formal interdiction or condemnation of confession by telephone in case of emergency, when death is near and it is impossible to call for a priest. Is there a sufficient doubt that the absolution could be validly given then, at least under these conditions? The confessor, in such an exceptional and urgent situation, must decide what to do according to his conscience.

We should always remember that we must work to achieve perfect contrition. Perfect contrition, which we may obtain from God through prayer, helps us regret our sins since our faults are a lack of love and manifest the weakness of our friendship for the Lord. Perfect contrition obtains forgiveness for our sins.

IS THE PENITENTIAL RITE OF THE MASS AS VALID AS THE SACRAMENT OF RECONCILIATION?

In the penitential rite of the Mass, the priest says: "May Almighty God have mercy on us, forgive us our sins and bring us to everlasting life". Is it as valid as the Sacrament of forgiveness? Is it only for venial sins?

* * *

We can obtain the Lord's forgiveness through an act of contrition. 'Perfect' contrition even obtains forgiveness for our mortal sins; such a perfect contrition of our serious sins comprises the will to confess them in the sacrament of reconciliation. The grave sins committed after baptism must be confessed: such is the teaching of the Catholic Church. The *Code of Canon Law* reflects the Church's position: "The faithful are bound to confess, in kind and in number, all grave sins committed after baptism..." (Can. 988, 1).

There are other ways than the sacrament to obtain pardon for our venial sins: acts of charity, prayer, expressions of our sorrow. Among these expressions, there is the penitential rite at the beginning of Mass. This penitential preparation helps us celebrate the Lord with a purified heart, a heart detached from all sins. It is worthwhile and precious, because in the words of the prayer we sincerely regret our faults; this is why it obtains remission of sins.

Confession, or the sacrament of reconciliation, is nevertheless a precious and necessary gift. It is a privileged way to receive God's forgiveness; it is an efficacious sign of his mercy: "Receive the Holy Spirit. For those whose sins you forgive, they are forgiven; for those whose sins you retain, they are retained" (Jn 20: 22-23). The sacrament of reconciliation remits our faults, gives us the Lord's help and fortifies us during our pilgrimage to heaven. It is necessary for those who fall into mortal sin: it is the suitable occasion to become reconciled with God. It is also most precious for those who have only venial sins. Confession remains a privileged road to conversion and holiness. This is the consistent teaching of the Church. Unfortunately, such a gift of God's love is not always understood and is not unwrapped often enough.

Let's make use of all the riches of the Church: works of charity, acts of sorrow, and the sacrament of forgiveness. God's love is given to us in so many forms. One of the most important is found in this sacrament.

WHAT ARE INDULGENCES?

What are indulgences? What are the conditions for gaining indulgences?

* * *

Paul VI, in his *Indulgentarium Doctrina*, the Apostolic Constitution on Indulgences promulgated on January 1, 1967, reemphasized the importance of indulgences and renewed their arrangement. On July 15, 1986, John Paul II issued a third edition of the collection of indulgenced prayers and works, the *Manual of Indulgences (Enchiridion Indulgentiarum)* adapted to the new *Code of Canon Law* (Can. 992-997).

These days, indulgences have been a bit neglected. They are primarily to help us strengthen our spiritual life.

On March 20, 1998, the Pope wrote:

"The truth of the faith and the practice of indulgences are directly linked to the Sacrament of Reconciliation. In effect, an indulgence is the remission before God of the temporal punishment due sins already forgiven ... The follower of Christ, with the proper dispositions and under certain determined conditions, may acquire it through the intervention of the Church.

Since the acquisition of a plenary indulgence first goes toward the detachment of the soul from its attachment to sin, it is a marvelous complement to the Sacrament of Reconciliation".

Indulgences are the manifestation of the mercy and love of the Father. The Sacrament of Reconciliation alone does not exclude enduring consequences of sin from which we must be purified. "With the indulgence given in relation to a repented sin, there is a remission of the temporal punishment for sins already forgiven". Thanks be to God, thanks be also to the communion of saints which unites believers to Christ and to one another.

ARE NOT INDULGENCES ANTI-LOVE?

Love cannot be bought or sold. We must be very ignorant about love to have invented such a system that seems so contrary to God's Word.

* * *

Let me clarify what is missing from the harshly worded statement above: a clear explanation of Church doctrine on indulgences.

It is true that love is not for sale. The Lutheran reform, for example, was against an indulgence granted for the material construction of a new Saint Peter's Basilica in Rome. The Council of Trent in the 16th century put an end to any further abuses and reaffirmed the legitimacy of indulgences.

Indulgences are not anti-love: on the contrary, they are a manifestation of God's love. They reveal God's goodness, his mercy, his ... indulgence. They never go against the Word of God. To gain an indulgence, certain conditions have to be fulfilled as indicated in the following paragraphs. Chief among them are the inner dispositions of the faithful, an openness to God's love, the exclusion of attachment to sin.

Indulgences are the remission, partial or total, of the temporal pain due to sins already forgiven (*Canon Law*, Can. 992-993). The Lord has entrusted to his pastors his divine power to forgive sins, to bind or to loose (*Catechism of the Catholic Church*, No 1478). Why should we object to indulgences? They are but a complement to the forgiveness of sins. The Church, when certain conditions are fulfilled, adds a total or partial remission of the temporal pain that sins already forgiven have incurred.

Civil courts may grant the remission of a punishment or change it into something else. The Church does the same for the temporal punishment due to forgiven sins. The indulgence offers a substitute for, or else totally abolishes the temporal punishment attached to sin.

To gain an indulgence, we must perform the prescribed action, for example we recite certain prayers, visit a church, console the sick, or give alms to the poor. For a plenary indulgence, we must also go to confession, receive Holy Communion and pray for the Pope's intentions. Good interior dispositions, such as remorse for our sins and love for God and neighbor, are always required.

Indulgences reveal God's love for us.

- VII -

THE SACRAMENTS (continued)

4. The Eucharist
   New order of the Mass
   Sunday Mass
   Eucharistic fast
5. Sacred Orders
   a. Priesthood
      Marian Movement of Priests
      Sermons
   b. Diaconate
      Deaconesses
6. Marriage
   Dissolution
   Marriage of homosexuals
   Common-law Marriages
7. Sacrament of the sick

WHAT ABOUT THE CONTROVERSY REGARDING THE NEW ORDER OF THE MASS?

There continues to be a great deal of controversy regarding the new order of the Mass. There are still those who believe that the revisions of the liturgical rites went too far. What do you recommend to those who prefer the former Mass with its deeper and more fervent prayers and reverent acts of worship?

* * *

The Mass contains liturgical rites that are essential and others of lesser importance. The elements originating directly from Christ, which the Church always jealously preserves, can never be abolished: the Word of God, the Offertory, the Eucharistic prayer, the consecration and communion. The Mass will always be a sacrifice and a divine banquet.

Some customs or prayers could be changed or had to be changed to allow the great Eucharistic prayer to be better understood and lived by the succeeding generations and the variety of peoples. A third edition of the new Roman Missal has come out in 2000; it was first published in 1969 and revised in 1975.

The Second Vatican Council made excellent improvements to the liturgical rites, in particular, those of the Mass. However, some people misinterpreted these changes and took them too far. We must distinguish between true liturgical progress and false adaptations. In striving to make the liturgy completely understandable, there is a danger of destroying that which is sacred and holy. The Mass is sacred; it is the divine liturgy and will always be beyond our human comprehension.

Some wish to keep, at all costs, the ancient traditions relating to the Mass and are still reluctant to accept change. Some even rejected the legitimate reforms which were implemented through the work of Vatican II; this rejection has resulted in some aberrations such as those of Archbishop Lefebvre.

Other Christians, both priests and lay people, wish to preserve the wealth of the past while continuing to remain faithful to the Church. For example, on the occasion of the tenth anniversary of the Motu proprio *Ecclesia Dei* (Apostolic Letter of John Paul II), in 1998, the Pope addressed a crowd of pilgrims. Present in the crowd were 2000 members of the 'Fraternity of Saint Peter', a movement faithful to the Church and to the ancient rituals. He used the occasion to invite "all Catholics to take action towards unity... and not allow the legitimate diversity and different customs, all worthy of respect, to separate them from each other". At the same time, the Pope wished "that all would come to terms with the spirit of Vatican II, in full harmony with the Tradition of the Church, and aiming at unity in the charity and faithfulness to the Truth". The Church, says the Pope, remains the faithful heir to Tradition as a living reality making progress for the benefit of the whole Church.

Cardinal Joseph Ratzinger was pleased with the positive results of *Ecclesia Dei*. He deplored the mistrust that surrounded the older rite. However, the existence of two rites does not necessarily conflict. Behind the two forms of celebration, there are two different spiritual standpoints. In the new liturgical rite, there is a lot of room for creativity and the active presence of the laity, because the liturgy is the concern of the entire Body of Christ. The older liturgical rite, faithful to sound Tradition, stresses the importance of the sacrificial nature of the Mass, the sacred mystery and the specific role of the priest.

More complete information on liturgical rites is contained in a conciliar document entitled: *The Holy Liturgy* and also in the *Catechism of the Catholic Church*, Nos 1322-1419. They urge us to be faithful to Tradition, yet open to progress.

WHAT ARE THE RULES FOR FULFILLING SUNDAY MASS OBLIGATIONS?

What are the rules for fulfilling Sunday Mass obligations? Is attending Mass on Sunday a must? I heard that masses attended before 4 p.m. on a Saturday don't count as a Sunday Mass. For example, I went to a wedding at 3 p.m. on a Saturday; am I obliged to go again the next day in order to obey the commandment of the Church?

* * *

We must not forget the importance of Sunday. Let us cherish the idea that during Sunday Mass, we celebrate the Supper of the Lord, Christ died and resurrected. On May 31st 1998, Pope John Paul II published an apostolic letter *Dies Domini (The Day of the Lord)* on the sanctification of Sunday. Sunday, he writes, reminds us of creation and the resurrection of Christ and we are invited to rejoice. Social and cultural changes do not alter the Christian significance of Sundays. We must give thanks together to the Lord by taking part in the Eucharist and spending a restful day in Christian joy.

The Church, since its origins, has always considered Sunday as the day of the resurrection, of the light, of faith, of hope, of the gift of the Spirit, of the table of the Word and the Body of Christ, of the Church, of fraternal gathering, of Christ's mission. The Eucharist remains the heart of Sunday. It is vitally important and necessary for one to participate, unless truly unable to do so.

There can be the Liturgy of the Word and Sunday gatherings in the absence of a priest, but nothing can truly replace the Eucharist. Masses on the radio or television help those people who are shut-ins or have serious difficulties getting to church, but they are no substitute for the celebration of the Eucharist for those who are able to attend Mass in person.

With respect to Saturday evening, Canon Law states: "The obligation of assisting at Mass is satisfied wherever Mass is celebrated in a Catholic rite either on a holyday itself or on the evening of the previous day" (Can. 1248, par. 1). Each diocese has the right to determine the hour at which 'evening' begins; commonly it is 4 p.m.

The Liturgical Calendar invites pastors to celebrate the day of the Lord's resurrection with zeal and joy. It states: "Wedding or funeral Masses are not to be considered as a Sunday Mass when they are celebrated on Saturday afternoon or evening" (1997-1998, p. 33).

However, according to an authorized commentary of Canon 1248, participation in 'any' Mass, even a wedding Mass, after 4 p.m., is enough to satisfy the obligation of Sunday Mass (*The Canon Law, Letter and Spirit*, The Canon Law Society of Great Britain and Ireland, 1995, Commentary No 2467, John M. Huels, O.S.M.). Remember, every Mass celebrates Christ's mystery.

Here is an exceptional situation, since nobody attends a Marriage Mass every weekend. And we should also keep in mind that the faithful going to a marriage Mass takes part in the celebration of two sacraments: the Eucharist and Marriage. The present interpretation, which is according to the spirit and not the letter, is still more acceptable when the faithful regularly attends Holy Mass on Sunday.

If after having participated in a Marriage Mass at 3 p.m. on Saturday, you think that you have fulfilled your Sunday obligation and you decide not to come back, you can be at peace.

WHAT'S THE USE OF GOING TO MASS?

What's the use of going to Mass? It's so boring!

* * *

You could be right! But maybe part of the problem is that our whole spiritual life is 'boring'...

I don't blame you. I agree that Mass is too often a lukewarm prayer, sometimes even cold. At times, it can be monotonous, with its symbols understood only by the initiated, homilies that have nothing to do with everyday life, with tedious or even non-existent hymns. Not always; not everywhere; but let's agree that it does happen.

It is unfortunate, especially in these modern times where television shows are produced with such flair by the media and other experts in communications and marketing.

Yet the Mass, even with the best modifications, can never compete with the sophisticated audio-visual world of secular entertainment. Above all else, the Mass connects with the depths of our souls, not only our emotions. The world of our souls is not the world of our human senses.

This does not mean that nothing can be done to make things better, that the presentation and participation in the Eucharistic prayer must always remain lifeless and dull. There is always room for improvement in areas such as welcoming, community participation, liturgy, hymns, dialogue and preaching.

But the Mass, "source and summit of our Christian life", remains the Mass, an indescribable mystery. It can never be understood without faith. Is it possible for such faith to grow in someone who is a reluctant participant in the Mass? Can faith rekindle itself in someone who does not go to Mass for various excuses?

Let's wake up our dormant faith! It is Christ himself who instituted the Mass (Lk 22: 19-20). Since the beginning, it has been the heart of the life of the Church.

Let's remember that the Mass is the Holy Sacrifice of Jesus, offered unceasingly to God, his Father, for our salvation. Through the Mass, the sacrifice of the cross is present and active. It is also the Supper of our Lord, a banquet of life which unites us to the divinity of Christ, by his Body and his Blood.

The Mass is our greatest Christian prayer. It is the prayer of Jesus, with Jesus, in union with the whole Church, the Mystical Body of Christ. Mass nourishes us with the Bread of the Word and the Bread of Life. The Mass gives us hope in eternal life.

The Mass is of such great importance that the Church obliges us to participate. "Sunday Mass is to be attended as well as specified feast days".

Our first duty as Christians is to praise God. No tribute pleases him more than the offering of his Son with whom we unite ourselves. Is it too much to give God one hour per week for the Mass, the Eucharist, also known as the Breaking of Bread (Ac 2: 42)? Especially on that day chosen by God – Sunday – the Lord's Day!

No personal prayer, no matter how beautiful, can equal the grandeur of the liturgical prayer of the Mass! Private prayer, whether individual or in community, may please us more, even create enthusiasm and enthrall us. But never can any such prayer have the infinite merit of the Mass!

This is true even if the Mass is celebrated without music, presided over by some poor priest lacking the gift of eloquence!

To understand this, we must refresh our faith. Gold remains gold, even though it may be covered with dust and dirt.

IS A CHILD OBLIGED TO ATTEND SUNDAY MASS?

My question is whether a child who is seven years old, and who has not yet received first communion, is obliged to attend Sunday Mass? When I was the same age, we had to attend Mass every Sunday and all holydays. Today, first communion is not until the third grade, along with the sacrament of reconciliation. In the Catechism of the Catholic Church, *nothing is mentioned on the subject.*

* * *

The *Code of Canon Law* is clear: "On Sundays and other holydays of obligation, the faithful are obliged to assist at Mass" (Can. 1247). Bound by the Sunday precept and other ecclesiastical laws, are all "those who were baptized in the Catholic Church or received into it, and who have a sufficient use of reason and, unless the law expressly provides otherwise, who have completed their seventh year of age" (Can. 11).

Elsewhere, the *Code* requires that children, who have reached that age, be prepared as early as possible for the Eucharist. "It is primarily the duty of the parents and of those who take their place, as it is the duty of the parish priest, to ensure that children who have reached the use of reason are properly prepared and, having made their sacramental confession, are nourished by this divine food as soon as possible" (Can. 914).

I am unaware of what motivated the decision in your parish to wait until the third grade for First Communion. There must have been valid pastoral reasons. My answer is the same, however: yes, a seven-year old child is subject to the Sunday precept, even if he or she has not yet received First Communion.

The example of parents should always be paramount. Parents who understand their Christian duty and the unique importance of the Eucharist will lead the way to Church, the House of God, for their very young children well before they reach the age of seven. Everyone knows that things we are taught at a young age will stay with us for life. Good habits are acquired very early.

Above all, parents should carefully explain to their children the reason for their actions and the significance of their religious customs. By their living faith, they will teach their little ones the value of praying to God, who is the source of everything good, of life and of its richness. We must offer him thanks through the Eucharist, along with other members of the Church's family, around the Table of the Lord.

Later, as they reach adolescence and are increasingly influenced by their peers and society, they might reject religious practices; but the seed of divine life will not die. One day, it will bear fruit, for the Holy Spirit is at work in the soul of every child. Parents are needed to assist the Spirit in his work.

DO WE STILL HAVE TO FAST FOR ONE HOUR?

My husband is 82 and I am 73. Do we still have to fast for one hour before receiving communion?

* * *

Here is the text from the *Code of Canon Law*: "Whoever is to receive the blessed Eucharist is to abstain for at least one hour before holy communion from all food and drink, with the sole exception of water and medicine" (Can. 919, 1).

"The elderly and those who are suffering from some illness, as well as those who care for them, may receive the blessed Eucharist even if within the preceding hour they have consumed something" (Can. 919, 3).

It would be an abuse of the law if we interpret this 'something' as a full meal; however, you can have something to eat before Communion, given your ages.

It is good, however, to remain ever respectful of the Sacrament and to reserve a little time for recollection and prayer before receiving Communion.

WHAT DO YOU THINK OF THE 'MARIAN MOVEMENT OF PRIESTS'?

What do you think of the 'Marian Movement of Priests' and the revelations given to Father Gobbi? Has the Church given pronouncement on the issue?

* * *

At times, the Marian Movement of Priests has received a negative press. Perhaps this is an opportune time to emphasize its positive aspects, by calling attention to the blessings received by so many bishops, priests, religious, thousands of laity, via the Movement that has deep roots in many countries.

To wisely discern the good despite the flaws, in any works where humans connect with the divine, one must not throw the baby out with the bath water.

To rebuke the Marian Movement of Priests, some put forth evidence of eschatological fears. Still, are we not to keep the invitation of the Gospel to convert and to ready ourselves?

We all can nourish ourselves with the spiritual 'vitamins' that come from the M.M.P.: a profound love of the Eucharist in living faith, a solid affection for the Virgin Mary and consecration to her Immaculate Heart, an unshakable attachment to the Holy Father and to the Church. I see numerous people who, in hundreds and thousands of cenacles (inner circles), in all the Christian universe, unite themselves as a family of the Church to pray, and resist as such the tidal wave of paganism. There, the faithful laity and members of the clergy fraternize, often weekly. The cenacles of prayer answer the real need in our Church for small fraternities where the Christian life is fervent and welcoming, a source of involvement and apostolate.

We should discern with our pastors and remain prudent. The 'blue' book is not a gospel; it does not pretend to be. The messages Father Gobbi has been conveying to us since 1972 are the echo of the words of the Virgin of Fatima. The Good News is spreading.

SHOULDN'T WE PRAY HARDER FOR OUR PRIESTS?

Instead of criticizing our priests, shouldn't we pray harder for them, that they remain faithful to Christ? God alone is the judge.

* * *

Jesus said: "Do not judge, and you will not be judged" (Mt 7: 1). So many of our judgments are based on outward appearances, on human standards (Jn 8: 15). Saint James questions: "Who are you to give a verdict on your neighbor?" (4: 12). Saint Paul adds: "So, no matter who you are, if you pass judgment you have no excuse" (Rm 2: 1); "You should never pass judgment on a brother" (Rm 14: 10).

All of these quotations, chosen from among many others, proclaim this law of the Gospel to us, that God alone is to judge. He alone probes our hearts and minds; he alone can read our inmost thoughts (Jr 11: 20; 1 Th 2: 4).

If God commands us not to judge so as not to be judged ourselves (Lk 6: 37), we must obey him. We should not give in to the feeling that we are better than someone else, to the temptation to behave as masters of the law and rescuers of doctrine and morals.

This is of particular importance with regard to the ministers of God, the priests, and especially the bishops and the Pope.

People who denounce doctrinal errors and moral deviations can be subconscious enemies of the Church. In wishing to eradicate the evil, they risk destroying the good; they threaten the overall unity and peace of the Church; they divide the Church and sow seeds of suspicion. They should leave the preservation of faith and good morals to those who are appointed and qualified to see to it. Priests are responsible to their bishop; the bishops work in the Church together with the Holy Father. Let us not become super-priests or super-bishops, much less super-popes.

Have there been situations among the clergy where, evidently, there has been disobedience to the authentic teachings of the Church and immoral conduct? Let us leave them to be dealt with by those who are responsible for them, usually their bishop or their religious superior. If necessary, let us voice our concerns to them privately. Afterwards, let us live in peace.

The Vatican decided to sponsor a conference on vocations in Montreal, April 2002. We must pray harder for our pastors, our priests. Those whom I know personally are a source of great strength to me. Their ministry is often thankless, difficult, judged from all sides and frequently seems to show little fruit. Pray for all of our beloved priests who are giving their lives to the service of the Lord and to the People of God. In our troubled world, they need our support, our affection, our encouragement and our cooperation more than our criticism, much more!

WHY DO PRIESTS' SERMONS PUT US TO SLEEP?

Mass is often dull for young people. Some priests have an effect like a sleeping pill. I despair in my frustration.

* * *

There are priests who put people to sleep; there are those who fall asleep; and there is a God keeping watch.

Let's not dramatize. Let's take action to make things better. It may be possible to help the priest, to offer our services in liturgical planning or music. Holy Mass is our shared responsibility.

Explain the value of the Eucharistic celebration to your children in a way that helps them to understand. Encourage them to appreciate this great prayer shared with Jesus and offered in the name of the whole Church.

Pray also at home and in prayer groups.

The Lord will do the rest. Your Christian example is of major importance for your children. May your serene and joyful attitude concerning Mass and the celebrant become contagious within your family and your community. This would mean so much!

WHAT DO YOU THINK OF THE PERMANENT DIACONATE?

What is your opinion concerning the permanent diaconate and the fact that certain dioceses are opposed to the ordination of permanent deacons?

* * *

The permanent diaconate was restored by Vatican II. The ecumenical council was in accord with the Tradition of the Church, going back to apostolic times (Ac 6: 1-6). Pope Paul VI published two apostolic letters to facilitate such a restoration: *Sacrum diaconatus ordinem*, in 1967, and *Ad pascendum*, in 1972. Under the influence of the Holy Spirit, the permanent diaconate has produced excellent fruits and facilitated a new evangelization. It has instilled a new life into Christian communities.

On February 22, 1998, linked by the same *Introduction*, two important texts for the training and ministry of deacons were published by Roman Congregations: *Fundamental Norms for the Formation of Permanent Deacons* by the Congregation for Catholic Education, and *Directory for the Ministry and Life of Permanent Deacons* by the Congregation for Clergy. There is need for a theological conception of the diaconate. It is important to clarify the mission of deacons and to define their human, spiritual, doctrinal and pastoral formation.

A permanent deacon "receives the imposition of hands and is strengthened by a specific sacramental grace which integrates him into the sacrament of order". Faithful to the Christian vocation, which is for all a call to holiness, the permanent deacon endeavors to resemble Christ, the servant of all (*Introduction*, Nos 4-5). Permanent deacons lead and liven up the ministry of service. They serve the People of God in the ministry of the liturgy, of the Word and of charity (*Lumen Gentium*, No 29).

The restoration of the permanent diaconate cannot be imposed upon any diocese (*Introduction*, No 16). All diocesan bishops should consult and decide whether or not the permanent diaconate ought to be restored in their diocese.

WILL THERE BE DEACONESSES ONE DAY?

* * *

The documents mentioned in the previous answer do not necessarily exclude women from the diaconate, but to the presbyterate and the episcopate. However, the Catholic Church invites only men to the diaconate. Vatican II stipulates that "this diaconate will be able to be conferred upon men of more mature age, even upon those living in the married state. It may also be conferred upon suitable young men" (*Lumen Gentium*, No 29). We find the same terminology in the *Code of Canon Law* (Can. 1024).

Numerous Christians, of both sexes, would like women to be ordained deacons. The Canon Law Society of America believes that the ordination of women to the permanent diaconate could be allowed; this seems also an opinion held among Orthodox. In April 1997, the first international congress for the diaconate of women took place in Germany. In November 1998, 73 % of the delegates in the Synod of Montreal voted in favor of deaconesses.

Of course, no such decision should be based on popular consensus, but rather on apostolic origin and motives.

Historical, theological and sacramental studies continue. What was the Church's attitude in the first centuries? Did women become deaconesses through the reception of a sacrament? The case of Phoebe in the letter to the Romans (Rm 16: 1), an excerpt from the first letter of Paul to Timothy (3: 11), and liturgical activities of the first centuries, are interpreted by some as a sign that there was a sacramental ordination of deaconesses, by others a simple religious blessing. In 1998, Bishop Saraiva Martins, secretary of the Congregation for Catholic Education, answered that there was no ordination of deaconesses.

Can we separate the diaconate from the priesthood and the episcopate? Here again, opinions differ: some say that the diaconate necessarily belongs to the sacred order with its three degrees: bishop, priest and deacon, and, therefore, must be conferred only to men;

others affirm that the permanent diaconate is not necessarily a step towards the priesthood and, therefore, can be conferred to women.

In 1987, Cardinals Danneels and Hume asked the Pope to reestablish the order of deaconesses. The door may not be hermetically sealed. Among those expecting further studies, I mention the members of a commission of the American episcopate, Cardinal Carlo Maria Martini, and many others.

CAN THE POPE DISSOLVE MARRIAGES?

The Pope himself cannot dissolve a marriage except in the case of adultery, of 'porneia', according to Saint Matthew. Why can't he do the same in cases of spousal abuse, verbal abuse, or incest? Is adultery the only sin, or is it a more serious sin than physical and psychological abuse?

* * *

Our Lord himself delivered a discourse on the principles of Christian ethics called the 'Sermon on the Mount'. He proclaimed: "But I say this to you: everyone who divorces his wife, except for the case of fornication (*porneia*), makes her an adulteress; and anyone who marries a divorced woman commits adultery" (Mt 5: 32). He said in another passage regarding marriage: "What God has united man must not divide... The man who divorces his wife - I am not speaking of fornication (*porneia*) - and marries another, is guilty of adultery" (l.c., Mt 19: 6. 9).

In the Catholic Tradition, the original word '*porneia*' means 'prostitution', or 'illegal union', to emphasize that it is a false marriage, a null or non-existent marriage that justifies separation and liberty to marry another.

It is not a question of one fault or another allowing for dissolution of a marriage. According to the unchanging teachings of the Church, based on the words of Jesus, a valid marriage, ratified and consummated, between two baptized spouses, can never be broken, not even by the Pope.

The Catholic Church has always maintained the indissolubility of the sacrament of marriage. She has never taught anything to the contrary, in spite of great pressure from the outside world, even monarchs. There are those who wish to soften the rules and expand the power of the Pope in these matters.

Based on the Word of God, the Church may 'dissolve' marriages that are deprived of sacramental character. For example, according to the 'Pauline privilege' (1 Co 7: 12-16), marriage between two non-baptized people may be dissolved in the case of one of them becoming Christian and the other refusing to continue living together (Can. 1143-1149). In another example, according to the 'privilege of faith', a marriage between a baptized person and a non-baptized person may also be dissolved. And the Supreme Pontiff can legally dissolve a marriage that was never consummated.

In other cases, where the marriage can be proved to have never been valid, it is possible to obtain a 'declaration of nullity'.

Even the Pope cannot change divine law, that which comes from God. The stability and indestructibility of such a Christian marriage have great value. A Christian marriage imitates the perfect union of Christ with his Church. "This mystery (of marriage) has many implications" (Ep 5: 32).

The Church cannot dissolve a ratified and consummated marriage between two baptized people, even in the case of adultery or some other fault. The *Catechism of the Catholic Church* reaffirms this teaching founded on the words of Jesus Christ (No 1644).

In the face of so many civil divorces in society today, it is a good idea to strengthen our knowledge of the teachings of Christ and the Church, at the same time avoiding to pass judgment on those who live, often with great suffering and bravery, in an irregular marriage. The Church invites us to imitate Christ and work to ease some of their anguish and heartache.

CAN HOMOSEXUALS MARRY ONE ANOTHER?

* * *

The Catholic Church doesn't believe that this is permissible nor should a same-sex couple adopt children. Not all human wants can be satisfied.

Denmark was the first country to give legal recognition to homosexual couples, in 1989; it was also the first to allow them to adopt children, at least those of their spouses. Other countries are moving in the same direction.

Marriage should remain an alliance between a man and a woman. It is better to use the terms 'marriage' and 'spouse' when referring to heterosexual couples, and speak of 'partners' when they are of the same sex.

Bishops are opposed to homosexual marriages. Such marriages are contrary to natural law and the Judaeo-Christian concept of life and marriage. Legislation in favor of same-sex marriages is the first step towards legalizing their right to adopt children. We can easily imagine the consequences for the society of tomorrow, if children are raised by parents of the same sex. Children of today already deal with difficult and confusing societal pressures as they develop their sexuality and they need the reassurance that natural law is still being upheld.

We have to resist certain pressure groups. This was the Pope's message to European leaders recently. What is at stake is too important. The Pope speaks of erratic tendencies concerning natural law. Speaking of same-sex couples, he used the word 'incongruity'. They cannot transmit life, according to God's plan. Moreover, in such relationships, the union of body and mind as planned by our Creator cannot take place.

Respectful of the Bible and natural law, the Church tells us that marriage is an alliance between a man and a woman, not between two people of the same sex (*Code of Canon Law*, Can. 1055).

WHY DO WE SAY THAT COMMON-LAW MARRIAGES ARE A COUNTER-TESTIMONY?

I accidentally read your web page as I was surfing the internet. You write about showing charity towards those living common-law: it is up to the person in charge, for example the pastor, to decide whether or not they could be involved in pastoral activities, for example serving at Mass, etc., since common-law marriages would be a counter-testimony to the Christian way of life.

Why do you say that common-law marriage is a counter-testimony? For what reason is it more so than say for a married couple who are having marital problems, malfunctioning, perhaps one of them is unfaithful or abusive (physically or morally)? Do you believe that God is not present in common-law relationships? How can we, from the outside, judge the intimate relationship between two persons? Is common-law marriage of less value in the eyes of God because it is not publicly instituted?

* * *

Man and woman are created in the image of God. "Male and female he created them... God saw all he had made, and indeed it was very good" (Gn 1: 27. 31).

The Bible often speaks of marriage. Marriage has its origin in God's plan revealed in the book of Genesis. God, states Vatican II, "is the Author of marriage" (*Gaudium et Spes*, No 48, 1). The New Testament tells us clearly that marriage is a sacrament which must reveal the alliance between Christ and the Church (Ep 5: 31-32). The *Catechism of the Catholic Church* echoes the beauty of Christian marriage (Nos 1601ss).

Christians are called to live according to the Gospel teachings. According to God's Word, the conjugal life must reveal God's plan for the couple. For a person who claims to be Christian, marriage is not simply a life with another person, a common-law marriage as we say. It must be an alliance open to love and life, which can only be ended by death, a covenant formed in the presence of God and of the Christian community.

The Church, which the Lord has founded, is in charge of the sacraments. If many Christians choose a common-law marriage, the Church respects their freedom of choice without approving their decision. Without passing judgment on their interior motives, she considers their life together as not fulfilling the requirements of the Gospel. I don't deny the presence of God in their love, but such Christians do not live as a couple according to the demands of Christian life. This is often due to ignorance and misunderstanding. The Church doesn't pass judgment on their intentions, but on their state of life. Therefore, it doesn't seem appropriate for pastors to ask them to participate in certain ministries when the way they choose to live their lives appears to be contrary to the teachings of the Church.

A couple married within the Church may indeed be in conflict, malfunctioning as you say, even unfaithful and violent. If their life is a counter-testimony to Christ's teachings, it is not for the same reasons. Their state of life is legitimate; their way of living is not what it should be. If it becomes apparent that their lives within their marriage have become a counter-testimony, it would also be prudent for their pastor not to have them involved in pastoral activities.

I AM LIVING IN A COMMON-LAW RELATIONSHIP. MAY I MAKE A VALID NOVENA?

Since I am not married, yet I live common-law, I don't receive Holy Communion because I am not allowed to do so. But, may I make a novena? Dear Father, I'd like an answer. I regret my situation which prevents me from receiving the Eucharist. But I love my companion with whom I have been happily living for the last twenty-five years.

* * *

My sincere congratulations for your spirit of faith and your fidelity to this man who shares your life! God, who is a God of mercy, will take this into account. Maybe you have children from this union. Keep praying to the Lord with confidence and love. Go to Mass, even though you may not receive the Eucharist.

If neither of you has been married before, and if you want to rectify your situation and get married sacramentally, please do not hesitate to do so. Speak to your parish priest about it.

Maybe one of you is separated or divorced; then, it would be good to verify if you could get a declaration of nullity for your previous marriage. If a declaration of nullity is granted, you would then be free to enter into a sacramental marriage, that is, a marriage before God and the Church. Here again, ask the assistance of your priest or of the diocesan pastoral services in your area.

If this solution does not apply in your case and if it is not an option for you and your companion to live separately, do not forget the possibility of living together like brother and sister. In prayer, everything becomes possible.

Make a confident novena. Good Saint Anne will listen to your prayer and will take care of you. I have no doubt that this novena will be helpful.

WHY IS THE SACRAMENT OF THE SICK RESERVED FOR THE ELDERLY?

Why is the sacrament of the sick reserved for the elderly? Being old is not a disease.

Why can't it be given to all who desire a spiritual, physical, or emotional healing?

What is the sacrament of the sick?

* * *

Jesus desires to perpetuate his healing gestures towards the sick, hence the sacrament of the sick... The anointing of the sick is the sacrament by which the Church recommends the faithful who are dangerously ill to the Lord, so he may raise them up and save them. She confers this sacrament by making the sign of the cross with holy oil on the sick and in pronouncing the prescribed words (Can. 998). One anointing on the body suffices for the validity of the sacrament; however, liturgical norms require anointing the forehead and hands as well.

The Church instructs pastors and those who care for the sick to keep vigil that they may receive the comfort of this sacrament at the opportune time (Can. 1001). The sacrament may also be administered in a communal celebration.

"Every priest, but only a priest, can validly administer the anointing of the sick" (Can. 1003, 1).

To answer your question regarding who may receive this sacrament, I quote the *Code of Canon Law*, the official legislation of the Church responsible for the sacraments: "The anointing of the sick can be administered to any member of the faithful who, having reached the use of reason, begins to be in danger of death by reason of illness or old age" (Can. 1004, 1). This sacrament may be administered more than once. And if the threat of a particular illness is questionable, the sacrament may still be administered, adds the *Code of Canon Law*.

We should prepare ourselves to receive this sacrament "with a faith-filled and devoted spirit", wrote Pope Paul VI in 1972 (*Sacram unctionem infirmorum*).

Old age is not in itself a disease, but the aged are often closer to death because of failing physical strength. Without hesitation, anyone "who begins to be in danger of death because of failing physical strength or by aging" may receive the sacrament (Paul VI).

According to the Tradition of the Church, the anointing of the sick is only done in the case of danger of death due to a physical weakness. Other prayers may help people who are suffering spiritual, emotional or mental troubles, in particular the sacrament of the Eucharist, with the presence of the risen Lord.

- VIII -

PRAYER

Popular devotions
Miraculous cures
The Way of the Cross

WHAT DO YOU THINK OF POPULAR DEVOTIONS?

* * *

Popular devotion is the devotion of the people of God. It springs from life more so than from doctrine. It is attached to celebrations, assemblies and festivities. It venerates Christian heroes, saints to whom the devotions confide. It believes in a God of all goodness, a God close to us, his children, and capable of intervening to help us.

Without such popular devotions, Christian life is at risk of being too cerebral, intellectual and cold. This is why we see Church pastors as well as the faithful laity praying popular prayers and participating in pilgrimages to shrines.

Paul VI and John Paul II, among others, praised popular devotions. The Pope prays his rosary and visits shrine after shrine.

Popular devotion does have certain limitations. It may be considered by some to be superior to learned devotion, that of the theologians. It is possible that this is reciprocated... It is a shame, as these devotions are there to complement and enrich one another. Never will one succeed in destroying the other...

Popular devotion must be centered on Jesus Christ, be nourished by his teaching and must not fall into pure and simple sentimentality. It must learn to discern, especially when something seems to be marvelous.

Long live popular devotion, that of my parents and millions of other Christians who, thanks to it, are sanctified, in faithfulness to Christ and his Church.

CAN WE BE PIOUS WITHOUT SOUND DOCTRINE?

Can we have the gift of devotion without sound doctrine or true discernment?

* * *

Sure! It's possible.

Some of the faithful readily listen to the words of pious and devout people as though everything they say is truth. That someone is holy does not necessarily mean that he or she is an expert in Christian doctrine. Devout people are not a substitute for learned people. They are even less comparable to the pastors of the Church who have been mandated by God to lead us towards him and guide us along the right path.

Pastors thus appointed are not always saints, but they, the Pope and the bishops, are the successors of the twelve apostles, who were given the mission to proclaim the Gospel (Mt 10: 14). It is the Lord himself who chose them. United with the Supreme Pontiff, the bishops form the Magisterium of the Church, and their mission is to authentically and officially interpret the divine Revelations.

Occasionally, fervent people are misled and sometimes mislead others by their teaching which is contrary to that of the leaders of the Church. I am thinking of pious people like Arius, who lived in the 4th century. I can also think of more recent examples, particularly in new religions.

"Those voices that proclaim themselves to be Catholic, and who give the impression of speaking on behalf of the Church, in reality are not" (Cardinal Roger Mahony, Archbishop of Los Angeles).

If you are still unsure, don't forget about discernment. One of the essential criteria for proper discernment is whether our devotion is faithful to Church doctrine, that which is taught by the Pope and by the bishops united with him. You can trust their judgment.

In the papal encyclical *Faith and Reason*, Pope John Paul II warns us against the danger of devotion and faith that disregard Church doctrine. He wrote: "Faith without understanding places emphasis on emotions and experience...". It is blind faith. This type of devotion runs the risk of weakening our faith by relying on superstition and human sentiment. These days, many people are wary of Church doctrine and mistakenly adopt these sentimental attitudes.

WHEN WE PRAY, AREN'T WE TELLING GOD WHAT TO DO?

When we pray, nine times out of ten we tell God what to do instead of asking for the grace to do his will. Who are we to tell God what to do and how? Shouldn't we rather concentrate on "thy will be done"?

* * *

I agree with you. We are a bit feeble-minded in our Christian life, anxious to receive and not so willing to give.

We forget that we must first strive to do what the Lord requires. We are poor children who stumble and fall, crying to God our distress. In our confusion, we want what we think we deserve: the end of a trial, success in our enterprises, a special favor for our children, cure of a sickness, or financial help. In our prayer, we dictate to God what he must do. If he doesn't obey us, we sulk, we reject him; we may even stop praying.

Poor people that we are! Our prayers are so fragile. Holiness consists in doing God's will, not ours. I regret that many of our prayers are for selfish and material desires, without sufficient confidence in God's providence.

We are blessed that our God is a God of love. He himself urges us to pray with trust. "Ask and you will receive, and so your joy will be complete", says Jesus (Jn 16: 24). He will grant what we ask, but he will often give us more than we ask for. Like all parents, he will never give us gifts that would harm us. Jesus says: "If you, who are evil, know how to give your children what is good, how much more will your Father in heaven give good things to those who ask him!" (Mt 7: 11).

When our suffering seems excessive, may our prayers resemble the prayer of Jesus during his agony: "Abba (Father)! Everything is possible for you. Take this cup away from me. But let it be as you, not I, would have it" (Mk 14: 36).

However, let's not be judgmental towards those who do pray for specific intentions. We are, all of us, God's children searching for happiness, and God understands it and shows compassion. When something painful happens to us or to a loved one, we too may cry in our anguish. God will listen. Is he not a Father full of tenderness?

MAY WE PRAY TO OBTAIN MONEY?

I'd like to know if it is suitable to ask Good Saint Anne for financial gain. If I win money, I will help sick children and people in misery. For the moment, I have no job. Is my prayer clumsy?

* * *

We are God's children. Our heavenly Father gladly listens to our childish prayers. Didn't Jesus do just that 2000 years ago? They rushed to him to obtain a cure, a favor. Jesus, full of kindness, listened attentively. He cured them, chased away evil spirits, pacified tormented souls, and did many other things that made them happy. But he didn't do anything for the sake of popularity, but just as signs to show them that God's Kingdom had come.

No doubt that you can make your requests to Saint Anne or directly to the Lord! Especially if your ultimate desire is to use the money to help people around you who are less fortunate. But also be resigned to God's will! Money can be a tool, but it can also be an idol. It is most useful when we share it with others. There are different ways to share: paying our taxes, helping raise funds for the Church, giving to humanitarian and charitable organizations, offering our tithes, etc.

To begin your petitions, ask for spiritual favors: love for God and neighbor.

Pray as Jesus told us in the Our Father, above all for what is essential: "Our Father, hallowed be thy name, thy Kingdom come, thy will be done!"

After that, you may present your own needs: "Give us this day our daily bread...".

The 'bread' you ask for includes material blessings, although the most important 'bread' is spiritual grace.

Prayer should be a loving conversation with God and the saints. It must not be limited to requests for material things; it must deal with what is spiritual: doing God's will, advancing on the road to holiness.

This doesn't exclude our requests for special earthly needs. We are not pure spirits. God urges us to pray: "Ask and you shall receive" (Mt 7: 7). He is aware that our material and corporal necessities are for us a source of worries; he doesn't take offence if we express our anxiety in our prayer. His disciples were never snubbed by him, even when they selfishly asked for the first place in his Kingdom. But he made them stop and think when he spoke of a cross to carry and invited them to become perfect.

SHOULD I WAIT TO PRAY BETTER?

This is not a question, but an observation and a suggestion. I tell the younger people: "Don't wait until you are older to pray better. For me, the more I age, the more I sleep. This is my problem".

* * *

Prayer, this is what nourishes our faith, our hope, our love of God and our neighbour.

Prayer, this is our duty as Christians who want to worship the Lord, to contemplate him, to adore him, to thank him, to ask him forgiveness.

Prayer, this is the expression of our need to God.

Prayer is necessary for people of all ages.

Now that you have reached a certain age, you humorously lead us to understand that you readily fall asleep when you pray. Then, sleep! The Lord rejoices in seeing his children sleep, just as parents smile with happiness watching their baby fall asleep in the crib. Offer your fatigue as a prayer; it will please God.

Of course, you understand that I don't suggest that you pray negligently, without attention, without fervour, without love.

One must reserve some time every day for prayer, especially in the morning and the evening. It is suitable to leave a place of honour for the great prayer of the Eucharist on Sunday. We must pray while working, to lift our hearts to God, to offer him our activities, our worries, our desires, to commend to him those who are dear to us. Don't forget, in your kindness, the immense needs of the Church and of the world.

Let us hear Jesus telling us: "Stay awake, praying at all times" (Lk 21: 36). Stay awake, that is, remain vigilant.

WHY DOES A PERSON WHO PRAYS A LOT SUFFER FROM NIGHTMARES?

Why does a person who prays a lot and receives communion every day suffer from nightmares (violence, hate, sexual deviance...)?

* * *

We can't stop nightmares by praying more or receiving communion often. Too many Christians have the impression, or the conviction, that if they pray a lot, their pain will necessarily go away, their suffering will end and that there will be paradise on earth. When this doesn't happen, they are scandalized, believing that God does not exist and that their prayers are therefore useless.

When we became Christians, we did not cease to be human.

Jesus did not promise us that we would live in constant sunshine if we became his disciples. He said to us instead: "Anyone who does not carry his cross and come after me cannot be my disciple" (Lk 14: 27). We must walk in his steps, carry our cross after him, to please him and imitate him.

Nightmares: who doesn't have them on occasion? They are part of our human makeup, perhaps the result of poor digestion or rich food.

These nightmares can contain scenes of hate and violence, dramatic situations in which we are involved without having a way out, without even finding a voice to call for help. We often wake up suddenly.

They can also sometimes contain erotic scenes. Are the dreams stimulated by any pornographic films or videos we may have watched? If the answer is yes, we are somewhat responsible for their occurrence. If not, then do not worry. Sin is committed in the volition, not in the involuntary unconsciousness of sleep.

WHY DO WE SEE SO FEW MIRACULOUS CURES?

Proclaiming the Good News, the laying-on of hands... Why do we see so few miraculous cures and healing?

* * *

Your question refers to the words of Saint Mark when the risen Jesus sends the Eleven out into the world on their mission (Mk 16: 15-18).

You claim that we see so few physical cures and, without doubt, you are right. Can we explain this by citing a lack of faith, trust or zeal these days? Isn't there room to grow in these virtues with an increased openness to the Lord and his Spirit? We are living in a time of skepticism and rationalism.

On the other hand, one must not only rely on visible evidence and results. 'Good fruits' and healing are not only of a physical nature.

I read the writings of a Mexican evangelist, Jose Prado Flores. He wrote that Saint John doesn't talk of miracles, but of signs. In this way, for example, by the multiplication of the loaves, Jesus gives us a sign that he is giving us the true bread from heaven, his body and his blood. Also, in bringing Lazarus back from the dead, he represents himself as the resurrection and the life. He himself is the great sign, the manifestation of his Father's love, above all, for sinners.

Healing occurs in hospitals and cures may be achieved through both traditional and alternative methods of treatment. Healing obtained from Jesus occurs to manifest the living Christ. Too often, we focus only on the restoration of our health or the possibility of a cure and we don't pay attention to salvation, the message behind the sign. Cures and other wonders proclaimed by Jesus are associated with evangelization. They must accompany the preaching of the Word. The Lord heals the body to heal the heart.

If the proclamation of the Word is accompanied by signs, such signs must be accompanied by the Word. Otherwise, they will hardly demonstrate the love of God, but be only a display of a charism.

The Church continues "the ministry of the preaching and the healing of Christ in the sacraments and through charisms", writes Father Rufus Pereira. Once again, it must be emphasized that the wonders of physical cures are only one aspect of our healing. The more important healing, is it not that of the soul? Physical cures do take place; we have only to think about Lourdes or Saint Anne de Beaupre to believe. In the process of beatification or canonization, the Church requires confirmation from heaven of the saintliness of a person by a miracle. These healings are not the result of any psychological autosuggestion, but are obtained through faith and prayer.

Even though God does not produce such wonders on demand, it does not mean that he does not exist. Physical healing is not a necessity, but is a grace that may be given to us by the Lord, always in order to increase our love for him.

WOULD YOU EXPLAIN THE WAY OF THE CROSS?

I don't really understand the eighth station, where the Lord says to the holy women: "Daughters of Jerusalem, do not weep for me; weep rather for yourselves and for your children" (Lk 23: 28).

* * *

Congratulations for making the stations of the cross! The Way of the Cross represents the infinite love Jesus had for us, as he gave himself up to die on the cross. It urges us to love him in return. Saint Alphonsus of Liguori, the founder of the Redemptorist community, was inflamed with love for the Lord as he meditated on his passion.

Not everybody can go to the Holy Land and walk in Jesus' footsteps. Ever since the Middle Ages, Christians made the stations of the cross in their own churches. Those who are sick and shut-in can do the same at home, holding a crucifix. The Way of the Cross is a meditation to love God and regret sins; it leads to holiness. We learn from Jesus how to carry our cross daily, uniting our sufferings to his. We may obtain his mercy and gain indulgences.

As we meditate on the stations of the cross, we contemplate the innocent Jesus as he suffered and died. At the eighth station, women weep over him. Jesus invites them to worry instead about themselves and their children.

Jesus is like green wood which shouldn't be burned; yet, he is mistreated and tortured to death. Sinful people are like dry wood, and, therefore, should fear even worse treatment. This is why our Savior has compassion for his judges and executioners.

If we live in sin, we should pity ourselves rather than Jesus.

- IX -

MARY

Devotion to Mary
Her virginity
Apparitions
Medjugorje

WHY SHOULD WE PRAY TO MARY?

* * *

Christian Churches are divided in regard to Mary, even though all venerate her. Catholics and Protestants love, respect and honor Mary. They try to imitate her.

The Mother of the Lord is invoked by the Orthodox and the Catholic Churches, but Protestants refuse to pray to Mary and to the saints.

The 'cooperation' of Mary to our salvation is a major bone of contention. For us, Catholics, we believe that the alliance between God and humanity originated in God. We also believe that this alliance became effective through our responsible answer, by our cooperation. Mary, the 'servant' of the Lord, has cooperated in a special way, in her unique role, accomplished in faith and obedience.

We have for her a special devotion, the Marian cult. This cult is not understood in the strict sense, since there is no cult but of God. But, according to a wide and well spread meaning of the word, we speak of a Marian cult, of prayer to Mary and to the saints. This is a cult of *dulia*, that is, reverence, not a cult of *latria* or adoration.

We praise Mary, as did Luther, Zwingli and many reformers. Mary said in her magnificat: "All generations will call me blessed" (Lk 1: 48).

We venerate Mary, we praise God for her presence and role as Jesus' mother, just as the angel did at the Annunciation (Lk 1: 26ss) and Elizabeth at the Visitation (Lk 1: 39).

If we have recourse to Mary and to the saints, it is to ask for their intercession. Strictly speaking, all prayer is addressed to God alone. Our prayer to Mary is ultimately a petition to God who alone may grant our requests. We pray to Mary and to the saints that they may intervene on our behalf.

"Holy Mary, Mother of God, pray for us, sinners".

The 'Groupe des Dombes', an unofficial ecumenical association in France, published a study showing the origins and development of Marian devotion and presents a more elaborate answer to this question.

WHY IS THERE SUCH DEVOTION TO MARY?

Why is there such devotion to Mary when the Lord tells us that we must worship God alone? Why do we pray through Mary? And how is it that she promises salvation in her apparitions even though no one but Jesus Christ can save us? I wonder if I am doing right in praying to the Virgin Mary.

* * *

Yes, you are, and the Church guarantees it.

Maybe, however, certain notions of faith should be clarified. The *Catechism of the Catholic Church* can help in this matter.

We must always remember that the Virgin Mary was a human creature like we are, the "handmaid of the Lord" (Lk 1: 38). She is the "temple of God, and not the God of the temple", wrote Saint Ambrose, who so loved Mary and preached about Mary in the fourth century.

But Mary, the first believer (Lk 1: 45), had a unique mission and became the Mother of Jesus, the Mother of her Lord (Lk 1: 43), the Mother of God, the theotokos (Council of Ephesus, in 431). She was "so highly favored" (Lk 1: 28).

The devotion we accord to Mary is not that of divine worship, it is the devotion of veneration. The Lord is not jealous of his Mother. He loves her as any normal child.

If she promises us salvation in her apparitions, it is always in reference to the salvation obtained through her divine Son, Jesus. He is our Savior. As Catholics, this is the essence of what we believe.

Mary, our Mother in heaven, also cares for us, her adoptive children. She intercedes for us. We have a powerful and good Mother in heaven. It's Jesus who wants it this way. What a gift!

DID THE VIRGIN MARY MAINTAIN HER VIRGINITY?

Did the Virgin Mary maintain her virginity when Jesus was born?

* * *

The words of the Creed: "Jesus was born of the Virgin Mary..." define one of the four dogmas concerning the Mother of Jesus: her virginity, her divine motherhood, her immaculate conception and her glorious assumption to heaven.

Belief in the virginity of Mary began in the early Church. The first praises of Mary focused on her virginity. We also know that the Fathers of the Church celebrated the virginity of the Mother of God. This can be found in the written works of Saint Ignatius of Antioch (d. 107), Saint Justin (d. 165), Saint Irenaeus (d. 202), as well as the saints of the Golden Patristic age: for example Athanasius (d. 373), Ambrose (d. 397), Jerome (d. 419), and Augustine (d. 430).

Mary, as does her divine Son Jesus, sets an example for all men and women who consecrate their virginity to the Lord and who live as ascetics, hermits in the deserts, or coenobites in cloisters. This in no way devalues the sanctity of the Christian marriage, which is a sacrament of Jesus Christ.

Mary is the most highly favored creature of God. She is the Mother of God, since she is the Mother of Jesus who is God. Her divine maternity explains all her other privileges.

Mary remained a virgin before the conception of Jesus, during his conception, and after it.

Holy Scripture leaves no doubt regarding the virginal conception of Jesus, work of the Holy Spirit: "She was found to be with child through the Holy Spirit" (Mt 1: 18-20); "The Holy Spirit will come upon you... So the child will be holy and will be called Son of God" (Lk 1: 35). Such is our faith!

We also believe totally in the virginity of Mary before Jesus' conception and afterwards, according to the unchanging Tradition of the Church.

Those who do not share this faith are quick to point out that the Bible contains references to brothers and sisters of Jesus. It is important to note here that among the Jewish people, in the Hebrew and Aramaic languages, the word for *brother* and *cousin* is the same word. When the biblical texts use the word, it can mean cousin as much as brother. The Catholic Church interprets scriptural references to relatives of Jesus to mean his cousins.

As Catholic Christians, we praise God for the virginity of Mary, the Virgin Mother. She is truly holy, of an unparalleled holiness among all creatures of God.

This explains her immaculate conception and her glorious assumption into heaven. The dogma of the immaculate conception was proclaimed by Pope Pius IX in 1854. The dogma of her glorious assumption was defined by Pope Pius XII November lst of 1950. "Mary is the first Pascal flower" (Normand Provencher, O.M.I.).

WHY DON'T WE TALK MORE ABOUT APPARITIONS?

Why don't we talk more about apparitions of the Virgin Mary all over the world? Why do they always seem to take place in Europe? Should we be suspicious that it is a trick? I heard that only the apparitions in Lourdes are authentic. Can we petition Mary to come and appear to us here in North America?

* * *

Contrary to the way the first question is worded, I think we speak about it a lot. The phenomenon of visions, apparitions and messages, is not new. We only have to look in the Old Testament and within the history of the Church. In the Middle Ages, the occurrence of apparitions and extraordinary marvels became more pronounced, especially connected with the mystics and saints who lived in that time.

To counter the rationalism of the 18th century, religious manifestations have increased in significance in the last two hundred years. Remember the Marian apparition at Guadalupe in Mexico in 1531; at La Vang in Vietnam in 1799; all those in France: the miraculous medal in 1830, La Salette in 1846, Lourdes in 1858, Pontmain in 1871; in Ireland: Knock in 1879; in Portugal: Fatima in 1917; in Belgium: Beauraing and Banneux in 1933; in Italy: Syracuse in 1953; in Japan: Akita in 1973; in Venezuela: Betania in 1976; to name but a few of the better known apparitions recognized by the Church. Because of its notoriety, Lourdes is the most famous. The messages from all these apparitions follow those of the Gospels and lead us to prayer, conversion and pilgrimages.

In these last years there has been an increase in apparitions, true or false, and not only in Europe: Garabandal in Spain, Medjugorje in ex-Yugoslavia, Kibeho in Rwanda, NaJu in Korea, and others in Equator, in Ukraine, etc. I do not list them all.

What should we think about these apparitions and rumors of apparitions? Should we deny that any of them are authentic, or believe them all? These are the two extremes to avoid. One must always discern, in light of the Word of God and the teachings of the Church. The Church shows great caution in case there is risk of false, even diabolical witnessing. There is always danger that superstition and attention to the sensational may mask true faith and belief. A naïve approach would repel many believers. The Church is particularly careful with respect to secrets and predictions about the future. We must discern with prudence.

We should never underplay the presence of Christ in the Word of God and in the sacraments. The Revelation ends with Jesus, Word of God. The Church, however, has the power to recognize the supernatural origin of an apparition and thus she can condone the worship and pilgrimages that follow. With regards to those visions not yet approved by the Church, caution is advised. If she rules against a certain apparition, she does so after much study and investigation, and it is wise to obey the Magisterium that originated in Christ. I remember the sad ending to the false apparitions in Pescara, Italy, in 1988, where 100,000 people were deceived.

True apparitions, often to ordinary children, should nourish us in our faith, and renew the call to serve others.

The following are two testimonies showing great insight into this matter.

Saint Alphonsus Mary of Liguori, Doctor of the Church, wrote: "Some, while flattering themselves that they are without prejudice, take pride in not believing in any other miracles than those recorded in the Holy Scriptures, and consider the others to be stories or old wives tales. But... as much as it is wrong to give credence to every story, it is wrong to reject miracles that are witnessed by serious and pious believers" (*The Glories of Mary*).

The Jesuit theologian Rahner went so far as to state: "One cannot see why one cannot believe in a personal revelation from someone who has experienced it and admits with sufficient conviction that it originated from God".

WHAT ABOUT THE MARIAN APPARITIONS AT MEDJUGORJE?

What do you think about the Marian apparitions at Medjugorje? After more than 20 years, the Church has not yet confirmed their authenticity. What do you think about the books on Medjugorje?

* * *

Medjugorje, I feel, holds a prominent place among recent apparitions.

The Church, it is true, has not made a definitive declaration regarding Medjugorje. Does she really have to, while the apparitions continue to occur?

On May 26th 1998, the Congregation for the Doctrine of the Faith decreed that the negative attitude held by the Bishop of Mostar was his own personal opinion and not necessarily that of the universal Church. At this time, the Church cannot confirm the supernatural aspect of these apparitions, but neither does she deny it. She entreats her bishops to favour a holy devotion to Mary. Cardinal Franjo Kuharic and other bishops from the country accept Medjugorje as a shrine, and investigations are ongoing. If 'official' pilgrimages under the full sanction of the Church cannot be organized under present circumstances, there is nothing to prevent Catholics from making a private pilgrimage to Medjugorje. Many bishops and priests have already done so.

Good fruits multiply.

The same assumptions cannot be made in regard to all supposed apparitions. Mirjana, one of the visionaries at Medjugorje reported: "I've heard of a good many of these apparitions, some of which occurred in America, where the Virgin is reported to have prophesized about disasters, floods and other things. I tell you that these are not the words of Our Lady. Our Lady is our Mother who loves us; she does not wish us to love her out of fear. She changes our hearts with her smile and with her love. We have nothing to fear, but we must place our lives in her hands. Our Lady wants us to think about how to live fully in the present, because who can predict where they will be even in the next ten minutes? Our Lady wants us to be prepared to return to our Lord at any moment".

WHAT IS THE ORIGIN OF THE ROSARY?

A dominican monk told me that it is wrong to believe that Saint Dominic received the revelation of the Rosary by an appearance of the Holy Virgin.

I would like to know the origin of the rosary which we recite these days. When did we begin to recite it? Did it start in Canada?

* * *

I have assembled these questions on the rosary. In the great religions, the rosary, or its equivalent, establishes an easy and concrete bond with that which is holy. It is found in Hinduism; also in Buddhism where we see a *mala* or type of rosary on the wrist of the Dalai Lama, the spiritual leader of people of Tibet; also in Islam where the Muslims recite the holy names of Allah on their *sebhaa*.

There are several types of rosary: the rosary of the Seven Sorrows, the rosary of Saint Bridget, the rosary of Saint Anne, etc., but I want to talk mostly about the most common rosary.

Many opuscules favour the pious recitation of the rosary. Pius XII said that the rosary was "the summary of all the Gospel". John XXIII, Paul VI and John Paul II, among many popes, praised the rosary. The rosary lets us proclaim the Creed, recite the Our Father, the Glory be to the Father, the Hail Mary.

Since the 15th century, as the result of Dominican Alain de la Roche's influence (around 1470), the vocal recitation of the rosary is accompanied by meditation. We contemplate, during the recitation of the rosary, the principal events of our salvation: the joyful , sorrowful and glorious mysteries of the life of Jesus and the life of Mary. During the recitation of the rosary, that is to say the rosary of fifteen decades, we relive all which the Lord Jesus has done for us; near him, we find his Mother.

During the recitation of the rosary, our thoughts turn towards our Mother in heaven. We ask her to intercede for us, "now and at the hour of our death". She leads us to Jesus.

What is the origin of the rosary? It didn't just happen all of a sudden, the result of an apparition, not even to Saint Dominic who made good use of the rosary. It comes from the Middle Ages, mainly between the 9th and the 13th centuries, but no precise date can be attached to it. Christians were already reciting the first part of the Hail Mary, using the inspired words addressed to Mary by the angel of the Annunciation and by Saint Elizabeth. The second part came from the Church.

Christians hailed Mary: Ave, Salve... This was the age of chivalry, of the invocations to Our Lady. Gradually, the custom of reciting 150 Hail Marys was established, just like the monks reciting 150 psalms. The Hail Marys were divided into decades; each decade started with the Our Father and, later, it ended with the Glory be to the Father. The recitation of the rosary became the breviary of people illiterate and devoted. To help in counting the Hail Marys, rosaries were manufactured with string. With devotion, Christians presented to Mary this circlet of flowers ('chaplet'), this garden of roses ('rosary').

The obscurity of the origin of the rosary is not very important, but we know the importance which the Church places in it and the richness it contains. In the time of Saint Pius V, at the end of the 16th century, the recitation of the rosary was widespread; one can attribute to it the victory of Lepanto, in 1571, over the Muslims.

The great writer, Charles Péguy, wrote:

"What I love in the rosary, says God,
it is that it is simple and that it is humble,
just like my Son,
just like my Mother".

- X -

SAINTS AND ANGELS

Halloween
Saint Anne
Guardian Angel
Statues

WHAT IS THE IMPORTANCE OF HALLOWEEN?

Halloween... I think this pagan celebration has been given more emphasis in today's society than any of the other Christian celebrations such as Christmas, Saint Valentine's day and especially Easter. I realize that it allows people to be creative and have fun. Children especially like to dress up. I also realize that the Unicef collection that night is for a worthy cause, although some Unicef projects have not been condoned by the Church. But perhaps we could place more emphasis on Thanksgiving Day to discourage Halloween.

* * *

There is a hierarchy in the importance of Christian feasts. The most important one is that of Easter, the feast of the resurrection of Christ, which marks the victory over sin and death. "If Christ has not been raised, you are still in your sins" (1 Co 15:17). All we have to do is to rise with him into true Christian life. "Since you have been brought back to true life with Christ, you must look for the things that are in heaven, where Christ is" (Col 3:1).

We like to celebrate that other great Christian feast, Christmas, when God became man, Jesus our Saviour. Unfortunately these days, for many people, Christmas is simply a commercial holiday; the emphasis is on material things.

Thanksgiving has a more recent origin. On one special Monday each year in Canada, or on one special Thursday each year in the United States, we are encouraged to praise and thank God for blessings received in the past year. You are correct to feel that this is important to do. And we have many other holydays, some of lesser importance, such as Saint Valentine's Day.

The origin of Halloween goes way back in history, and variations are found in different countries. For example, for the Celts (Irish, Scots...), it was a celebration of the dead, who were thought to wander about as spirits and to whom one offered food and drink. The Church was opposed to these customs, which seemed to be diabolically influenced. The commercial way Halloween is celebrated these days does seem to overshadow other Christian holydays, and great financial profits are made from the sale of treats, costumes and decorations. Children dress up and go 'trick-or-treating' door-to-door.

October 31st, Halloween, is the eve of the Feast of All Saints. 'Hallow' means blessed, as we say in the Lord's Prayer: "Hallowed be Thy name". Parents can use Halloween in a positive Christian way to teach their children about the celebration of the saints in heaven and remind them that it is also a special time to think of our dearly departed whose feast (All Souls' Day) is celebrated on November 2.

It is also an opportune time to do a good deed, to help needy children by donating money to the UNICEF boxes that are around for Halloween. UNICEF is the only United Nations agency financed by private donations and the most important international organization dedicated to children. However, as a point of caution, in recent years, UNICEF has participated in activities involving global population concerns and the plight of women, specifically issues of abortion and the use of contraceptives. The Holy See has reacted and requires that donations from Catholics be used solely for noble and approved objectives.

WHAT IS YOUR OPINION ABOUT REVELATIONS CONCERNING SAINT ANNE?

Maria Valtorta, in her writings, places Saint Anne's death before Christ's birth, whereas another servant of God, Anne Catherine Emmerich, faithful to her visions, speaks differently. She even says that Saint Anne married again after Saint Joachim's death. She relates a visit to the crib by Saint Anne, who was accompanied by her second husband and the sister of the Blessed Virgin. Where is the truth? What do you think of revelations concerning Saint Anne?

* * *

The Bible is silent about Saint Anne and never mentions her name. Does this mean that we know nothing about her?

Don't we already know the essential facts: that she was Mary's mother and Jesus' grandmother? Isn't this all we need to think about in order to praise her, love her and pray to her? This is the reason why Christians in every century and in all countries have revered her. We still venerate and invoke her. She was indeed so close to the Virgin Mary and to Jesus, our Savior. Besides, she is the link between the Old and the New Testament.

Apocryphal books mention Saint Anne and describe some of the events of her life. Although these books are not divinely inspired like the books of the Bible, what they say concerning Saint Anne is not pure fiction. Apocryphal books go back to the first centuries of the Church, especially *James' Protogospel*, which may have been written during the first century, certainly not later than 150 A.D.

The apocryphal books were very popular. They have been mentioned in the writings of the Fathers of the Church and numerous saints; we shouldn't be any more skeptical than they were... These books were inspired by information that had been orally passed down through the years. The stories nourished the piety of generations of believers and they continue to do so today. They inspired great artwork: paintings, sculptures, mosaics, stained-glass windows... They must be respected.

In the course of history, certain saints received revelations concerning Saint Anne. The Church does not require our faith in such revelations. Visions and spiritual messages that come through holy people are worth our respect. If their stories happen to be different, these differences do not call into question the holiness of their writers nor their honesty. God permits each one to consider certain details of Saint Anne's life to be authentic, even though they differ from other alleged visions. Each writer is influenced by his or her own knowledge, experiences and temperament. The essential facts don't change: Saint Anne, Mary's mother and Jesus' grandmother, deserves our love and trust.

Don't worry if Anne Catherine Emmerich says that Saint Anne's death occurred later than the time mentioned by Maria Valtorta, or if she mentions that Saint Anne married three times, a fact which is rejected by the majority of religious scholars.

Venerable Maria d'Agreda and Saint Colette also had revelations concerning Saint Anne. Their writings are not identical, yet it does not create any problem.

Continue your prayers to Good Saint Anne, knowing that because she is close to Jesus she is powerful, and being a grandmother she is kind. She will intercede on your behalf; she will pray with you to her Grandchild Jesus.

CAN YOU EXPLAIN HOW NATIVE PEOPLE HAVE SUCH A DEVOTION TO SAINT ANNE?

* * *

We live in a time of controversy and accusations between native and non-native people in Canada, and yet, precious dialogue continues with our native brothers and sisters. In 1999, the Canadian Council of Catholic Bishops published a pastoral message to Catholic members of the First Nations; they represent almost half of the 550 000 native people in Canada. The bishops reminded them that their traditions are a treasure of the Church. There are many holy people in their ranks. Can we forget the example of Blessed Kateri Tekakwita, the Lily of the Mohawks, who died in 1680, or the edifying life of Rose Prince, of the Carrier Nation in British Columbia, who died at the age of 34 in 1949? The Church acknowledges and respects the abundance of good and holy elements in their culture. This includes their very old devotion to Good Saint Anne.

As I travel around preaching devotion to Saint Anne, I visit many Indian reserves. Many of their churches are dedicated to her. I often find statues and banners in honor of Saint Anne: at Eskasoni,

Big Cove, Burnt Church, Waycobah, Indian Brook, Lennox Island, Bear River, Chapel Island, Barra Head, Wagmatcook, Millbrook, Pictou Landing, Red Bank, Listiguj, etc., among the Micmacs; in Kingsclear, Tobique, Woodstock, among the Malisseets; in Old Town, Maine, among the Penopscots; etc. It is moving to see how attentive the chiefs are during the ceremonies, also the many fervent men and women, young people, even the children who sneak among pews and who are proud to carry shades and candles for the procession.

Devotion to Saint Anne is popular all over North America, in the east as in the far north and out west, for example at Lake Saint Anne, Alberta.

Every last Sunday in June, the Shrine of Saint Anne de Beaupre celebrates the First Nation Sunday. Natives come from all over, the Hurons-Wendats, the Micmacs and Malisseets, the Algonquins, the Montagnais, the Abenaquis, the Attikameks, the Mohawks, the Naskapis, the Ojibways, the Crees, etc. They celebrate the Lord in the Eucharist, they gather at the foot of Saint Anne's statue, they take part in the candlelight procession, they express their faith in traditional Indian rites: the sweet grass ceremony, the dance of the crops, etc. After Mass, bishop, priests, chiefs and organizers, dancers and members of the choir, share together a banquet offered by the Redemptorist community in charge of the Shrine.

Devotion to Saint Anne goes back to the time of the first missionaries, diocesan priests, Recollets, Capuchins, Jesuits, and communities of Sisters. Coming from Europe, these apostles were moved by a deep devotion to Saint Anne. Native people immediately loved her and venerated her. In 1610, the great chief of the Micmac Nation, Membertoo, was converted. The Micmac nation became the eldest daughter of the Church in North America. Thanks in part to its devotion to Saint Anne and in spite of great difficulties, the Micmac nation remained faithful to Christ and to the Catholic Church. The other First Nations did the same. Some chose to be buried at Saint Anne de Beaupre. The first organized pilgrimage to the Shrine of Saint Anne de Beaupre was made by the Huron nation in 1671.

What happened in Canada also took place in the United States. Thanks to Father Carheil, a Jesuit who was cured by Good Saint Anne, the Cayugas, of the Mohawk family, developed a tremendous love for Saint Anne, Mary's mother and Jesus' grandmother.

Father Curtis Sappier, a young priest of the Malisseet Tobique First Nation, in New Brunswick, presided over the Eucharist at the 1999 First Nation Sunday at Saint Anne de Beaupre. In his homily, he said:

"Our ancestors have always told us: 'Respect your elders'.

This is a teaching we truly respect and uphold as native people,
    when we take the time to listen
    to their stories as we drink of tea,
    when we take the time to learn
    our old ways as we cast our lines to fish,
    when we take the time to love
    as we gaze at the rising sun our Creator has given us.

As Christians, we need to remember our ancestor Saint Anne.

When adoring the Lord or honoring his Mother,
let us not forget the ancestor, Grandmother Saint Anne".

IS IT PROPER TO TALK TO YOUR GUARDIAN ANGEL?

I named my Guardian Angel 'Raphael'. He watches over me and protects me. Is it proper to talk to your Guardian Angel? It gives me great comfort to do so!

I bought books on guardian angels, and enjoyed reading them very much, but my family is concerned about the truth in what the authors are writing. I don't want to distort my spiritual development with ambiguous information.

We have a scrapbook on angels. We give them names. We wear little angels as brooches and as necklaces. We collect angels for a hobby...

* * *

These questions and comments are all about angels, a popular trend these days. However, our Christian belief in the existence of angels has nothing to do with the present New Age focus on angels.

We believe that the primary duty of an angel is to adore God. Guardian Angels watch over us, help us and guide us towards God. In faith, we discover the marvels of the spiritual world. We do not deny the existence of the supernatural, in particular the celestial angels; and also Satan and his fallen angels who have genuine but limited power.

Angels are often mentioned in the Bible, both in the Old and New Testaments. Yahweh, our God, "will put you in his angels' charge to guard you wherever you go" (Ps 91:11).

Jesus himself speaks often of angels and the role they play in salvation. Even the littlest ones, the poor, the children, have angels who watch over them (Mt 18:10). We must not scorn them. The Church continually encourages us to ask our Guardian Angel for help.

There are many references to angels in the *Catechism of the Catholic Church*. The existence of angels is a truth of faith (No 328) that the Tradition of the Church has always endorsed. In our secularized world, we shouldn't deny their existence, the way the Sadducees did in the time of Jesus. There is a hierarchy among the angels. They contemplate God and are his messengers. As they were present in Jesus' life, so also they are present in the life of the Church. Saint Basil wrote: "Every faithful has a Guardian Angel".

Anything you might read that is in conflict with the teachings of Scripture and the Church should be put aside, in particular some recent New Age publications on angels. In this spiritually deprived world, it is too easy to make idols of secular 'angels' with magical powers. Some writings even border on the occult.

Angels work for God, not for our own selfish or earthly desires. They are not God, nor his equals, but are superior to us in their perfection. They protect us and intercede for us. Don't confuse your

Christian faith with eccentric viewpoints. Be careful about supposed personal revelations that encourage a spirituality and practice foreign to that of Holy Scripture and the Tradition of the
Church, for example mediums who claim to contact angels through
'channeling'.

Don't buy books on these subjects; it is a lucrative market. Even
if there are similarities between the New Age information and
Church doctrine, there are also significant differences to be aware
of. Angels are always creatures of God. They are never self-suffi-
cient beings.

Belief in the existence of angels is not a central element of our
faith, says the Pope; however, they do have a role in the history of
our salvation. Among the better-known angels are Michael, Raphael
and Gabriel.

Let us ask our Guardian Angels to protect us from harm, to
help us and to guide us in our journey towards God. Speak to them
in prayer.

WHAT DO YOU THINK ABOUT STATUES?

*What do you think about statues? In the Bible, God warns us
not to worship idols. He says there is no life in statues, that
there is only one way to heaven and that is through Jesus Christ.
Scripture says: "their idols... have mouths, but never speak, eyes,
but never see..." (Ps 115: 5)*

And why the crucifix?

* * *

When we read the Bible, we must always search for what the
inspired writers wanted to tell us. Otherwise, if we neglect common sense, we may make mistakes in our interpretation. Each biblical writer had his own style, his own literary genre, personality
and human limitations.

The Scripture quoted in the question is an excellent example. The Hebrew people, surrounded by pagan nations, slipped easily into idolatry. Yahweh reminded them that he was the one God, that man-made objects are simply that, and are not the Creator. And in the ten commandments, he entreats his people so inclined to superstition, not to create false images or statues that would lead them to idolatry (Ex 20: 4; 34: 17, Dt 4: 16, etc.). "Through human vanity they came into the world" (Ws 14: 14).

Nevertheless, it is this same God who ordered that two cherubs be forged in beaten gold, to place near the throne of mercy in the sanctuary (Ex 25: 18). This very God commanded Moses to fashion a bronze serpent (Nb 21: 8-9). The serpent was not a god. "Whoever turned to it was saved, not by what he looked at, but by you, the universal Savior" (Ws 16: 7).

The Church has always taught us to avoid idolatry. She opposes the practice of fetishes and amulets to bring good luck or to ward off evil. Nevertheless, she has always accepted statues and images that help us to adore the Savior himself, to venerate the Virgin Mary and the saints. She holds in honor the crucifix, which reminds us of the infinite love of Christ who died for our salvation.

God became visible to the human eye, coming among us in the form of Jesus. Why not remember him with the crucifix, pictures, icons and statues? "The Church has not only the right but the obligation to show what God himself has revealed to us" (Lucien Coutu). The crucifix that illustrates the love of God who died to save us has a prominent place in the homes of many Christians.

In the Oriental Church, icons play a significant role, representing God, the Mother of Jesus, angels and saints. To put an end to iconoclasm (the destruction of images and icons), the Church officially proclaimed the legitimacy of images and statues (Nicaea II, in 787). It is not that we must adore these human-made objects; he who venerates the icon, venerates that which the icon represents.

Don't we keep photographs of our loved ones in special places around our homes and workplaces? Is this idolatry?

- XI -

FAITH

Works or faith
Psychology and faith
Faith, hope and charity
Our conscience
Spiritual direction

WOULD YOU ANSWER MY QUESTIONS BY PERSONAL CORRESPONDENCE?

I like your question box as you preach retreats. It prompts me to question my faith and my beliefs, etc. Are you available to answer my questions personally?

* * *

Unfortunately, I do not have enough time to give personal answers to the numerous questions asked me in person, by letters or by email.

There is another reason that I cannot answer individually. Delicate questions are often asked to me concerning morals or personal problems. To answer without knowing all the details and discussing the problem thoroughly, I risk taking the wrong approach and giving an inappropriate answer.

I do keep all of the questions I receive in a file, and I try to give objective answers that may help not only the questioner, but also others who have similar concerns, and I publish my replies in magazines and books or on our web page (http://www.cssr.net/repchret).

My answers try to avoid a case-by-case approach. As I present the theological background for sound judgment, I do my best not to give simplistic answers to our complex and dramatic human problems. Within the words, I present values and I suggest Christian attitudes to take. My answers are inspired by the teachings of Jesus and of the Catholic Church. The reader must retain responsibility for his/her decisions.

ARE WE SAVED BY OUR WORKS OR BY FAITH?

In the Bible, the good thief on the cross believed in Jesus. Jesus said to him: "Today you will be with me in paradise". That guy was a bandit and Jesus forgave him because he believed. We are not saved by our actions, but by our faith. Faith is God's gift (Ep 3: 8-9). Do you agree?

* * *

The Bible affirms that the repentant sinner will be welcomed in God's heaven. We read: "But if the wicked man renounces all the sins he has committed, respects my laws and is law-abiding and honest, he will certainly live; he will not die" (Ez 18: 21).

The fate of a righteous person who sins is quite different; he may not expect the same happiness. Scripture tells us: "But if the upright man renounces his integrity, commits sin, copies the wicked man and practices every kind of filth, is he to live? All the integrity he has practised shall be forgotten from then on; but this is because he himself has broken faith and committed sin, and for this he shall die" (Ez 18: 24).

The good thief repented; Jesus promised him heaven the same day. His faith in Jesus, as you say, saved him. Nothing is said concerning the bad thief.

I agree with you that faith alone saves us, and you are right when you add that faith is a gratuitous gift. "Because it is by faith that you have been saved, through faith; not by anything that you have done, so that nobody can claim the credit" (Ep 2: 8-9).

Yet, good works are necessary: the result of our free and personal response to the faith received.

A few years ago, Catholics and Lutherans reached an agreement concerning justification by faith, which was a bone of contention and a fundamental controversy. Still not everything is clear and studies must continue. The Catholic Church teaches that divine mercy enables us to cooperate with grace, but that man may refuse such help (The Council of Trent, DS 1554). God's grace doesn't depend on man's actions, but justification is impossible without man's cooperation.

Listen to Saint James: "Take the case, my brothers, of someone who has never done a single good act but claims that he has faith.

Will that faith save him? If one of the brothers or one of the sisters is in need of clothes and has not enough food to live on, and one of you says to them: 'I wish you well; keep yourself warm and eat plenty', without giving them these bare necessities of life, then what good is that? Faith is like that: if good works do not go with it, it is quite dead" (Jm 2: 14-17).

WHY CAN'T WE COMBINE PSYCHOLOGY AND FAITH? ARE THEY NOT BOUND TOGETHER?

* * *

There are two pathways to knowledge: one through natural reason, the other through divine faith. This is the teaching of Vatican II (*Gaudium et Spes*, No 59). They are not incompatible.

Psychology is human reasoning, with human interpretations. It is a branch of philosophy that has become a specific science: the science of the nature, functions and mentality of the human soul or mind.

"Faith is a gift of God, a supernatural virtue infused by him" (*Catechism of the Catholic Church*, No 153). Faith opens a perspective that goes beyond what our natural intelligence can grasp. Faith is to accept a gratuitous revelation of mysteries the human mind cannot know: the Trinity, the Incarnation, the Redemption, the reign of God, the wisdom of the cross, etc.

Faith accepts, at their level, the just conclusions of psychology. Theology may make use of sound conclusions for a better understanding of faith.

Psychology in its pure form is not contrary to faith.

Nothing prevents us from combining psychology and faith; on the contrary! Faith does not despise science; faith does not exclude reason; faith does not exclude psychology. "Though faith is above reason, there can never be any real discrepancy between faith and reason" (*Catechism*, No 159).

Psychology does much to help us understand human behavior. Why should we reject it? Why should we dissociate psychology from faith? Does not psychology come from God, from the same God who gave us both, intelligence and faith? Both are necessary; the two must respect each other. For a more detailed discussion, I refer you here to the Pope's brilliant encyclical: *Faith and Reason* .

WHAT IS THE RELATIONSHIP BETWEEN FAITH, HOPE AND CHARITY?

* * *

Many spiritual men and women have written about these three great virtues. They are called theological virtues because they unite us to God. They are the most important virtues because they relate us directly to him. Faith unites us to God, as we know him by his divine revelations; hope unites us to God, as we wait with confidence for the blessed moment when we will enjoy his presence in heaven; charity unites us to God through our love for him.

FAITH in Jesus Christ is what makes us Christians. It is a gift from God and also an act of free will on our part. Our human intellect, under the influence of our will and God's grace, accepts the revealed truths because of God's authority. If these revealed truths are put forward by the Church, our faith is catholic.

Our faith is the foundation of our supernatural life and is a source of holiness, because it nourishes us with revealed truths. As long as our 'spirit of faith' is strong, then faith will always be our light, strength and comfort. It can weaken and become polluted by sin and widespread untruths promoted in some literature, in New Age practices and beliefs, etc. Our faith is nourished through prayer and by devout living. Faith grows in stages throughout our lives, developing over time. Faith produces good fruits. True faith will be contagious and evangelize.

In HOPE we wait for the blessings of heaven and the means to reach it. Its strength originates from the power and love of God. Christian hope comprises our desire for that happiness which is God himself and the confidence to attain it.

Hope sanctifies us by drawing us closer to God. We pray with confidence and we become more devout. It protects us from the temptation of false gods. Hope sustains perseverance and gives strength through hardships, even unto martyrdom. Our hope is also sustained by our contemplation of the Lord who is so good and compassionate. It puts despair and presumption to flight, while we trust in God, not simply relying on our own strength alone. Hope can produce a sense of childlike abandon as we see in the life of Little Theresa.

In CHARITY, we love God above all things; in charity, we also love our fellow man. Charity is sanctified love. Charity makes us love God, the Good, the Beautiful, the Wonderful *par excellence*, and to love human beings created as his children in his image. Our charity is limitless and grows with our efforts helped by grace. Charity also develops over time and bears many fruits.

The virtue of charity sanctifies us. It will always exist. Charity unites us to the Lord and transforms us in him. It banishes sin. It makes us desire to do the will of God. It makes apostles. It is nourished by prayer, contemplation and action. It creates the saints, the martyrs, the mystics, the missionaries, all those who are saved. The love of God is accompanied by brotherly love that forgives, sympathizes and sacrifices.

"In short, there are three things that last: faith, hope and love; and the greatest of these is love" (1 Co 13: 13).

IS THE VOICE IN OUR CONSCIENCE
THE VOICE OF GOD?

* * *

Such a delicate question! The answer can be tricky. We can readily oppose the voice of our conscience to the voice of the Church. Especially in the controversial doctrines dealing with birth control, abortion, euthanasia, freedom of expression of the theologians, the ordination of women, etc.

Freedom of conscience is not without restrictions; it must respect the truth. Freedom is not an absolute which becomes the source of values, the Pope tells us. The encyclical *Veritatis splendor* (*The Splendor of the Truth*), published August 6th, 1993, states the danger to watch for in freeing our consciences of all constraints.

God shows us the way to him: the observance of his commandments. The beatitudes also suggest behaviors and attitudes. It is not up to the individual's conscience to decide, in an autonomous manner, what is good or bad. The conscience is not infallible. We must search for the truth. "Do not model yourselves on the behavior of the world around you", Saint Paul tells us (Rm 12: 2).

Acting this way, we preserve human dignity and moral law. Faith includes ethics. Moral doctrine and conscience are not enemies of each other.

In our world where individualism reigns, some use their conscience to believe what they want. They are allergic to dogma and authority. Ethics, for them, consists of doing what they please. Based on their uninformed conscience!

Paul VI and John Paul II were constantly vigilant against subjectivism. The encyclical *Faith and Reason* warns us that contemporary intelligence does not search thoroughly enough for the true values, but seeks refuge in the pragmatic.

We were created free, but accountable. We must listen to the gospel, to our pastors, to the truth.

We must always follow our conscience, but clarified and forti-fied by moral doctrine. Christianity has something to tell us: hu-man reasoning must always yield to the reasoning of God; it's for the best.

WHAT'S THE DIFFERENCE BETWEEN A SPIRITUAL DIRECTOR AND A CONFESSOR?

* * *

A confessor and a spiritual director could easily be one and the same person.

All confessors should give spiritual direction. They direct the penitent along the road to conversion and holiness. Of course, they may not be able to give much detailed direction due to time con-straints and limited knowledge of their penitents.

This is one of the reasons why we make a distinction between these two ministries: that of the confessor, who gives absolution for our sins in the sacrament of reconciliation, and that of the spir-itual director who provides appropriate guidance in spiritual ways.

You may be aware that in our day and age, laypersons - women as well as men - act as spiritual directors. They can be very good at it. This is quite acceptable as long as these laypersons have the proper preparation in theology and spirituality. Of course, they cannot be confessors as they did not receive the priestly ordina-tion.

The role of the confessor is very important: he is the proxy of the Lord who went about forgiving sins while he walked on earth, and who transmitted the same power to his legates, the priests (Jn 20: 22-23).

A spiritual director also has a divine mission: to guide souls through what may seem to be the labyrinth of spiritual life.

To each one of us, God says: "Put out into deep water..." (Lk 5: 4). A confessor invites the soul to break the moorings and cast off. A director is the experienced pilot who leads the boat through the channel into the deep sea of holiness; he makes sure the soul will arrive in heaven safe and sound.

WHAT CAN I EXPECT FROM SPIRITUAL DIRECTION?

* * *

Spiritual direction may take place through personal dialogue or in a group setting. I will focus here on individual spiritual direction.

To begin with, may I point out a statement of fact: our era is one of 'democratic' holiness, that is many people live their Christian life their own way, without being attentive to Jesus' teaching. It is extremely important that we avoid amateurism, a Christian life which is not serious, not well-grounded in matters of faith, and the risk of regrettable consequences. We must pray and accept that all things are from God: desolations as well as consolations, suffering and joy, as we proceed on our way to eternity. Discernment is of primary importance.

Your spiritual director should journey with you, helping you by sharing his insight, and yet without playing the role of a psychotherapist unless he is qualified. He will engage you in compassionate dialogue, patiently listening to what you have to say rather than lecturing to you. He should not be verbose. A spiritual director should respect God's freedom, that of the Holy Spirit, also your own liberty. His job is comparable to that of a midwife, says Louf, knowing that it is not his duty to give life, but God's.

He will acknowledge the different stages of your spiritual life and will counsel you according to where you are on your journey to a greater Christian love. He will not offer simplistic answers to your questions, and avoid rationalization. His advice will be inspired by the Word of God, as well as the teachings of the Church.

He should remain detached from any extraordinary charisms and presupposed mystical phenomena you may have experienced, and he should stress what is essential: that you become the living image of Jesus.

Quoting Saint Paul, he should remind you: "Do not model yourselves on the behavior of the world around you, but let your behavior change... to discover the will of God and know what is good, what it is that God wants, what is the perfect thing to do" (Rm 12: 2).

- XII -

CHRISTIAN LIFE

Consecrated life
Contemplative life
Fervor
Scruples
Dreams
Charisms
Prayer groups
Neo-Catechumenate Way
Christian witness

WHY DOES THE CHURCH MAKE IT
AN OBLIGATION TO PRONOUNCE VOWS?

Why does the Church make it an obligation to pronounce vows, which are so like oaths? Saint Peter swore that he would give his life rather than betray Jesus. To take an oath like he did seems to be a sign of pride.

* * *

Vows are not oaths as expressed in the question. "A vow is a deliberate and free promise made to God, concerning some good which is possible and better" (Can. 1191ss). "A vow is an act of devotion in which the Christian dedicates himself to God or promises him some good work" (*Catechism of the Catholic Church*, No 2102). The Tradition of the Church, far from condemning such a practice, always praised it. Religious and other consecrated persons pronounce vows in order to better live out the Gospel.

Vows may be private or public, solemn or simple. "A vow is public if it is accepted in the name of the Church by a lawful Superior; otherwise, it is private. It is solemn if it is recognized by the Church as such; otherwise, it is simple" (Can. 1192).

Saint Peter failed to keep his promise to Jesus that he would not betray him; and he repented. His weakness, caused by a certain pride in his own strength of character, does not weaken the value of legitimate oaths, nor of vows or promises made freely, with God's help.

IS RELIGIOUS LIFE STILL MEANINGFUL?

* * *

The Conference of major religious superiors published a document about the spiritual riches of Institutes of consecrated life and of Societies of apostolic activities.

The latter, the Societies of apostolic activities, do not require religious vows; they accomplish an apostolate, they share a fraternal life and work to achieve perfection in conformity with their constitutions (Can. 731).

The former, the Institutes of consecrated life, live either a coenobitic life, in other words, they live in community; or else, an eremetic life, a life of solitude.

Besides, there are those who choose to remain celibate, living a consecrated life in the world.

Finally, there are new mixed communities, composed of men and women, and familial communities made up of whole families.

The Church remains constantly open to the action of the Spirit and discerns his action.

There are many praiseworthy ways of Christian living: priesthood, religious, lay. The Institutes of consecrated life have a rich history in the Church. They include the Secular institutes, approved in 1947 by the Constitution *Provida Mater Ecclesia*, whose members live in the world and work at its sanctification.

Since the beginning of the Church, many Christians were anxious to follow the Lord more closely, not only with the offering of their activities, but also with the total gift of themselves. They wanted to imitate Christ as fully as possible while serving the Church. They grouped themselves into religious communities to better practice the evangelical counsels of chastity, poverty and obedience; they pronounced public vows, temporary or perpetual; they were active or contemplative. Their consecrated life, lived in mutual love, prophetically heralds the world to come (Can. 573ss). Religious life has not lost its meaning and value!

Religious life is not a hierarchical structure of the Church, but the Church cannot forsake such a factor of holiness. Religious life is a charism of the Church. Its members identify themselves with Christ as they live chaste lives, in poverty and obedience. To tread the path of the evangelical counsels is to stroll on a privileged road towards Christian perfection.

CAN YOU EXPLAIN THE CONTEMPLATIVE RELIGIOUS LIFE?

* * *

The religious who live a contemplative life hold a special place in the Church; they are the heart of the Church, they give oxygen to the Church. They praise the Lord, they lead a holy life, they give an apostolic fecundity to the Church, they are a spiritual nuclear power.

On May 13, 1999, with the Pope's approval, the Roman Congregation for Institutes of consecrated life and for Societies of apostolic life published an Instruction on the contemplative life and the cloister of contemplative nuns, called *Verbi Sponsa*. This document, a masterpiece, stresses the value of contemplative life. As did the Pope in *Vita consecrata*, the Congregation stresses the necessity of remaining faithful to the cloister, be it the papal cloister, stricter and established by the Holy See, or the cloister set up by the Constitutions, which authorizes some apostolic or charitable activity.

Cloistered contemplative nuns and monks imitate Christ who prayed on the mountain and hung in self-denial on the cross. The cloister materializes the exclusive union of contemplative religious with Christ their Spouse, their unconditional love. Thanks to the cloister, the contemplative nuns and monks separate themselves from the world to better meet God in an exterior and interior desert. The cloister proved to be an important component in the sanctification of religious. Contemplation too! It is increasingly difficult to achieve solitude and contemplation in our noisy world of mass media and high technology.

Thanks to the cloister, contemplative religious are free to adore, praise and intercede. It is a foretaste of heaven.

Contemplative religious life is relevant today, more than ever!

WHAT CAN I DO TO BECOME MORE FERVENT?

What can I do to become more fervent? The will is there, but perseverance is not my strong point...

* * *

Saint Alphonsus invites us to pray every day for perseverance, to obtain it each day.

What should you do to become more fervent? Ask for this grace from the Lord. Fervor depends on him, on his help, not on our own will and childish efforts.

Pray!

Unwrap those numerous gifts we have received from God that we might resemble him in the fervor of our Christian life:

– the gift of divine life that was given to us at our Baptism, nourished through prayer and the sacraments, in particular, Reconciliation and the Eucharist;

– the gift of doctrine which comes through the Holy Scriptures and the Tradition of the Church, interpreted for us by the pastors of the Church;

– the gift of the Virgin Mary, of all the saints in heaven, always ready to help us;

– the gift of our brothers and sisters who journey with us, who support us, encourage us and assist us along the way;

– the gift of divine inspirations which, without fail, move us ever forward to salvation.

Our Lord, who calls us all to fervor and holiness, is always with us. We often think we journey alone, without God. However he walks beside us, is interested in what interests us, in what we have to say (Lk 24: 17). But what do we talk about on the road? Of ourselves, of our personal anxieties, or about him?

Give yourself up to the will of God, with his help.

He is the gardener of our lives. He wishes everything to be beautiful.

He wants to use us to proclaim the Good News. Like the disciples of Emmaus, he wants us all to return to Jerusalem, to the Church, to our sisters and brothers, to proclaim with joy that, in spite of suffering, he is alive!

HOW CAN I MAKE PROGRESS IF I AM SO FULL OF SCRUPLES?

I am a scrupulous person. I participate in the Eucharist often. I don't want to fall back into my old ways. How can I make progress if I am so full of scruples? Sometimes thoughts against God come into my head and I can't get them out of my mind. If someone does hurtful things to me, it eats away at me and I think vengeful thoughts. And so many other things disturb me.

How do I proceed at confession? Do I have to mention these things? Is it all right to confess without a full confession?

* * *

Scruples create problems as Christians struggle to live exemplary lives.

They are 'rough pebbles' that cause people to limp, and impede their march along the joyful road to God. It is excessive worry that convinces certain souls, that they have offended God. Scrupulous people confuse the imagination and consent. Scruples may have a physical cause, a sort of nervous depression; this disorder produces unfounded convictions that a sin has been committed. It may also arise from a moral source: a desire for perfection, misguided or ill defined, a pathological belief in a merciless God. When the causes are both physical and moral, they create greater obstacles to healing. Scrupulousness may also be a period of purification permitted by God; it could be a spiritual ordeal.

There may be scruples about everything, but also specific scruples on particular issues: past confessions, bad thoughts, blasphemous thoughts, lack of respect for the Eucharist, etc.

Scruples can be more or less serious; they are often only temporary.

Scruples should not be identified with the sensitivity of the conscience. Many saints manifested a hypersensitivity of conscience: in their complete love for the Savior they searched to avoid the smallest fault. The sensitive souls willingly submit to their confessors or spiritual directors.

A period of scruples may offer the opportunity to grow in humility and obedience. A scrupulous person should seek and strictly follow the advice of a spiritual director. May spiritual directors do their best to gain the confidence of a person who suffers from scruples, and once trust is established, to exact obedience (Tanquerey).

In the matter of your confessions, follow the advice of your confessor. Perhaps he will invite you to make a confession without detailing all your faults. With respect to communion, continue receiving it often.

SHOULD OUR ACTIONS BE INSPIRED BY OUR DREAMS?

I don't know what to think about a recent trend in personal formation where direction and decision-making are based on the interpretation of dreams. There is a warm friendship among participants.

* * *

Many people are curious about the significance of their dreams. They try to analyze them. They would like to draw conclusions and use them to better orient their life.

Dreams can be examined seriously. In many cases, we can trace their origin and learn something interesting about ourselves. How much are dreams a part of our subconscious? What are the reasons for our dreams?

People would like to discover God's will through their dreams. They read the Scripture passages relating the dreams of Isaac, Jacob, Joseph "the man of dreams" (Gn 37: 19), the Pharaoh, Solomon, Daniel and Saint Joseph.

God revealed himself in dreams which he interpreted himself (Gn 40: 8). But we must beware: dreams can be misleading. God blamed prophets for deceiving people with their dreams (Jr 23: 32). The meaning of dreams may be ambiguous.

Too many people are led by their imagination. Their dreams become fantasies, illusions and utopia. This makes them vulnerable to superstition and a false sense of right and wrong. A warm feeling of friendship in a gathering is not proof that the doctrine being discussed is authentic. Some grow rich at the expense of gullible and naive believers.

Protestants, as well as Catholics, are cautious when interpreting dreams. We must always refer to discernment, to common sense, to authentic doctrine, to the criterion of good fruits. We would be rash to organize our life according to our dreams. We must base our decisions on the Word of God, well interpreted by our pastors.

WHY DOES THE LORD GRANT CHARISMS TO UNWORTHY PEOPLE?

It is not necessarily a sign of God's love or sanctity to have charisma. Why does the Lord grant charisms to unworthy people and not just to those persons who seek God and their sanctification?

* * *

I cannot second-guess the wisdom of God, which is infinitely beyond me. In his divine liberty, he grants these gifts to whoever he wishes. Unfortunately, some do not use it to better love him.

At the moment of baptism, we all receive 'sanctifying' gifts. These gifts are a sign of God's friendship. If they are lost through mortal sin, they can be regained through a sincere confession of our sins, by our return to the friendship of God.

We have all received 'charismatic' gifts. We received them from God to enable us to help our brothers and sisters and to build the Body of Christ, which is the Church. We can and we must help one another.

But it does not necessarily mean that those who receive charisms are in a state of grace. One would assume that they would live in the faithfulness of God, but it isn't always the case. Also, Jesus warns us to be on our guard: "Many will say to me, 'Lord, Lord, did we not prophesy in your name, cast out demons in your name, work many miracles in your name?' Then I shall tell them to their faces: I have never known you; away from me, you evil men!" (Mt 7: 22-23).

These persons of iniquity had charisms, but acted sinfully. They prophesied, cast out demons, performed miracles, but they lived in sin.

Let us ask the Lord to help us make proper use of our own charisms, no matter what they are. Let us ask especially to love the Lord and to be faithful to him. Charisma must always be practiced with humility, in the love of God and neighbor. The great pathway to God is that of love (1 Co 13).

WHERE CAN I TURN TO IN TIMES OF DEPRESSION?

Where can I turn to in times of depression? I have older children who no longer practice the faith.

* * *

Too many parents are like you, in anguish and feeling fatigue caused by nights of insomnia. What can I tell you? Where do you find comfort, if not in your faith in a God who is love, in a Lord who came to earth not only for the righteous but also for the sinners, in a God who loves you and your children?

He does not want to lose even one soul; he does not want your children to be lost.

He loves them very much. He loves them more than even you love them!

Do you not believe that he will see to the good of your children, to their future, their eternity?

Ask him to take good care of your dear children. Ask this also of Mary and Saint Anne.

Trust!

HOW DO WE HANDLE DISCORD WITHIN OUR PRAYER GROUPS?

If, in a prayer group, there is a brother or a sister creating trouble or disturbing the assembly, must we expel them from the group?

* * *

Three cheers for imperfect groups! The poorest spiritual people, the anawim of Yahweh, the beginners in Christian life, Christians weak in their faith and awkward in their prayers can feel at ease within such groups. Wonderful are members of a group moved by Christian charity!

Returning to the question... The problem could be caused by a troubled mind and seriously jeopardize the order of the group. Not only could this irritate people, it could also create a serious obstacle to prayer and harmony.

Then, what can be done? It is left to the group leader to reach the appropriate decision, after careful consultation of the core group.

It may not be necessary to expel the troublemaker; it may be enough to warn him or her about the problem. In some cases, the leader or delegate may politely ask this person to remain silent for a while. Might it be better to ask him or her to leave the group, at least temporarily? This would be an extreme solution, only to be reached if there is no alternative to maintaining the peace.

An example would be if someone proclaims false doctrine, rejects authority, or divides the community. Desperate times call for desperate measures!

Normally, a simple warning is enough and a healthy group dynamic is restored.

Let's also be aware that some participants may wish to expel some people from the prayer group with whom they disagree.

Charity and good order must prevail, with respect for those in charge.

WHAT IS THE NEO-CATECHUMENATE WAY?

* * *

The Neo-Catechumenate Way was founded in 1964 in Madrid, Spain, by two laypersons, Kiko Argüello and Carmen Hernandez, and is made up of about 15 000 communities in almost 5 000 parishes in more than 100 countries. Its members do their best to understand and fully live an authentic Christian life, with the help of a program of formation similar to that of the primitive Church, yet adapted to baptized people and meant to last for years. We may say that the Neo-Catechumenate Way puts into practice the document *De catechesi tradendae* and is one of the fruits of the Second Vatican Council.

Our Holy Father has high praise for the Neo-Catechumenate, but in some countries, France and England, for example, its members are accused of creating a division within and of organizing activities parallel to those of dioceses and parishes. We must remember that the Neo-Catechumenate Way is rooted in parishes, contrary to other movements such as Opus Dei (a personal Prelacy founded in 1928 by a Spaniard, Blessed Josemaria Escriva de Balaguer), the Focolari (founded in Italy by Chiara Lubich in 1943), Communion and Liberation (founded in Milan by Msgr Luigi Giussani in 1954), and L'Arche (founded by a Canadian, Jean Vanier, in 1964).

Members of the Neo-Catechumenate Way may be guilty of certain human weaknesses. In certain parishes where we find the Neo-Catechumenate, some parishioners, who are not members, have the impression that they are considered as second-class Catholics, that their baptism was only a formality and that their Christian formation is considered incomplete. They regard the Neo-Catechumenate Way as a separate Church within the Church.

During the first gathering of ecclesial Movements held in Rome in 1998, which included the Neo-Catechumenate Way, Cardinal Ratzinger declared that new Movements might suffer from infantile sicknesses, but that such illnesses are curable. He added that these Movements belong to the Church and are a gift to the Christian community; local Churches cannot claim an absolute uniformity in their organizations and pastoral programs (May 27, 1998).

The Neo-Catechumenate Way appears to be providential and truly an action of the Holy Spirit, especially in light of so much de-christianization and religious ignorance even among the baptized in today's Church. It should be welcomed with joy and trust, in spite of possible friction, such as I mentioned above.

Kiko Argüello said to John Paul II in 1998: "Our faith must reach maturity and be significant to modern man and woman... Paul VI gave us his approval and said: 'You do, after baptism, what the primitive Church did before baptism...'. As for you, Your Holiness, you have said: 'I recognize the Neo-Catechumenate Way as an itinerary of Catholic formation valid for this time and for modern society'. Keep helping us in this apostolate which is beyond our means".

Like his predecessor, John Paul II has often praised the Neo-Catechumenate Way. He said one day: "I greet you with affection, brothers and sisters who dedicate yourselves to a very important task in the eyes of the Church: the edification in faith of an ecclesial community with the help of a systematic, solid and progressive catechesis. Give yourselves wholeheartedly to this necessary work; be faithful to the personal experience of the Christian message and transmit it to others. I bless your resolution to act in intimate communion with your pastors. I also bless your ministry, your persons, your families and your ecclesial communities".

HOW CAN I BE A CHRISTIAN WITNESS IN OUR MATERIALISTIC SOCIETY?

* * *

This answer cannot be a long treatise on testimony and evangelization.

To be a witness means to have seen, heard or perceived something.

To be Jesus' witnesses, we must believe in him, know him, and above all love him.

To be Jesus' witnesses, we must burn in our heart for him, of a bright fire, glowing, sparkling and warming.

To be Jesus' witnesses, we must let him fan our interior flame with his Word, the Eucharist and our prayer.

To be Jesus' witnesses, even unto death, we must be strengthened by the Holy Spirit.

The Holy Spirit will supply us with means and charisms to be Jesus' witnesses. As he did for the apostles of all centuries.

Many people no longer believe. Our mission is beyond our human capacities. But we are not alone: God abides in us. He is kind enough to make us his witnesses and to use our humble talents to proclaim the Good News.

At the time of the Roman Empire, of the Barbarians, of the Renaissance, in every century, Christians passed on the Christian message to generations which did not seem to be ready to accept it. The situation today is no different. The Spirit of God hasn't changed: it is as powerful as ever, in ourselves and in those who listen to us.

The Pope proclaimed that the 20th century was a century of martyrs, therefore of witnesses. According to the Pope, the 20th century had its own martyrology. We must study it and make it known. The Pope asks all bishops to pay special attention to the list of martyrs... They gave a great testimony to Christ. They sent a powerful message. Through their lives, they revealed that the world is in need of such 'fools of God'. And they included Christians of all denominations.

Mary still prays and obtains the blessing of Pentecost. Thanks to the Holy Spirit, we become daring witnesses, ready to be persecuted "in the cause of right" (Mt 5: 10), hopeful that our sacrifice will bear abundant fruits. It is our duty to be Jesus' witnesses, in our family, in our parish and where we work or relax.

- XIII -

ECUMENISM

Christian unity
Born of a Muslim father
Should I open my door?
How can we defend ourselves?

IS THE ECUMENICAL MOVEMENT MAKING PROGRESS?

* * *

Work for the unity of Christians makes some people very impatient. Others despair of success, because the obstacles seem insurmountable.

Christians all together have adapted to the ecumenical movement; they look for ways to better work for ecumenism; they retain hope. In the past, awkward attempts failed and aggravated the divisions within the Church. As much as we are to avoid proselytizing, which is an excessive zeal to convert other Christians to our faith, we must also avoid confusion concerning doctrine and religious indifference.

By its *Decree on Ecumenism* (*Unitatis Redintegratio*), issued on November 21, 1964, Vatican II revived the ecumenical effort. In 1967 and again in 1970 a *Directory* was issued to orient these activities. Progress was made. Agreements were drawn up and new documents were published. The new *Code of Canon Law*, in 1983, and the *Catechism of the Catholic Church*, in 1992, are two significant works.

Following these developments and to stimulate enthusiasm among all the faithful, Pope John Paul II approved the *Directory for the Application of Principles and Norms on Ecumenism*, on March 25, 1993.

The *Directory* examined the bonds between the mainline Churches; they have mutual respect for one another. It does not, however, include the many sects that abound worldwide. These sects reject all efforts of ecumenism. Their problem is extremely complex, as outlined in a 1986 publication from Rome.

The *Directory* established the theological basis for ecumenism, putting an ecumenical structure of the Church into place, especially with regard to the formation of all people in ecumenical action, outlining the correct spiritual dimension of ecumenism, and encouraging ecumenical initiatives.

On May 25, 1995, the Pope published an important encyclical on ecumenism: *Ut Unum Sint*. Christ prayed that his people be one and that all would believe in him (Jn 17: 21). Without destroying the diversity of spirituality, of discipline or liturgical rites, this unity should be a visible communion of all disciples of Christ.

This unity, gift of God, already exists in the Catholic Church governed by the successor of Peter and the bishops in communion with him (*Lumen Gentium*, No 8).

Through the ages, dissension divided the Church; the causes of these divisions are diverse and complex (*UR*, No 3). Since then, some Oriental Churches are not in perfect communion with the Church in Rome, even though we share the same ecclesiastical heritage that goes back to the first centuries. Similarly, the Reformed Churches (Protestant) have been isolated from the Catholic Church since the 16th century. We must reestablish complete unity as desired by the Lord. However, it can only be realized through prayer, conversion and by living a holy life; such is the soul of ecumenism, 'spiritual ecumenism', as decreed in Vatican II.

Ecumenical collaboration in present times occurs in pastoral work in hospitals and prisons, in the Armed Forces, and in the world of communications. Collaboration is a visible testimony for missionary activity worldwide. Should we not unite to fight against atheism, materialism, and the emergence of sects? Such collaboration should take place in our secular life, in all areas of social and ethical concerns, in all things that affect the poor, the dignity of women, refugees and immigrants, ecology, genetics, and mass media.

WILL THERE BE A CHRISTIAN UNITY?

I predict that, in years to come, there won't be any separate religions. There will be Christian unity, a unique gathering. What are your thoughts on this matter?

* * *

Let's not take our dreams too far. Religion, a collection of beliefs and dogmas, which unites man to God, will always exist. There will always be practices and formal rituals for this or that religion or Church. The Catholic Church founded by Christ will survive forever.

We can envision one Church, which would be the assembly of all Christians. This would symbolize a rediscovered unity, a unity longed for by our Lord. I wish it would happen!

Such an assembly, such a unity, seems humanly unachievable, so deeply rooted are the differences. Only the Holy Spirit can accomplish the miracle of unifying Christians. We must pray for this.

All throughout history, people wanted to know how to create one 'spiritual Church', beyond the barriers of beliefs, which many say are secondary in importance. Are these beliefs truly secondary? Because they are not, every effort to disregard them has succeeded not in creating a unique spiritual Church, but in establishing a new denomination, in addition to the denominations already in existence.

Although different, diverse Christian denominations lay claim to the same Christ and Lord. Unless the Lord unites us all in faith, I do not believe in the possibility of a re-assembly, in which all denominations would no longer need to exist. Let us pray that such unity will one day occur among Christians, when Christ wants and in the manner he wants.

WHAT CAN WE DO TO BRING ABOUT THE UNITY OF CHRISTIANS?

* * *

At the level of the whole Church, there is guidance for our actions in the area of ecumenism. There is the Pontifical Council for Promoting Christian Unity and the Pontifical Council for Interreligious Dialogue.

At the diocesan level, the bishop must designate a competent person and a diocesan ecumenical commission to move forward on ecumenical activity. This commission may draw members from more than one diocese if necessary.

Priests and faithful must make inquiries and learn about ecumenism. It is important that future priests and permanent deacons understand what is at stake in the unity of Christians and that they become well informed in the field of ecumenism.

Baptism incorporates us into Christ and his Church; it creates a sacramental link between all Christians. Why not recall our common baptism that unites us when we pray with other Christians?

Communion with other Christians already exists, even if it is imperfect. We can experience this communion when we pray together, for example during the Week of Christian Unity, in preparation for Pentecost or at other times.

We can rejoice in the action of the WCC (World Council of Churches). It groups more than 300 Christian denominations: Protestants, Anglicans, Orthodox, etc. Women play a major role in the assembly. Although the Catholic Church is not a full member of the WCC, Catholic members take part in various commissions and have delegates at the assembly as observers. The WCC celebrated 50 years in existence in 1998.

The other Christian Churches possess gifts: the Word of God in Scripture, certain sacraments such as baptism and the Eucharist, a life of grace, faith, hope and charity, etc. Yet, Vatican II affirmed that: "only through Christ's Catholic Church... that they can benefit fully from the means of salvation" (*Decree on Ecumenism*, No 3).

The Church founded by Jesus "subsists in the Catholic Church, which is governed by the successor of Peter and by the bishops in union with that successor, although many elements of sanctification and of truth can be found outside her visible structure" (*The Church*, No 8).

Ecumenical dialogue must continue at all levels, especially by the experts. Irenism, a false ecumenism based on a superficial peace, must be avoided. Doctrine must not be reduced to a common denominator.

TO ACHIEVE ECUMENISM, SHOULD WE TOLERATE ALL OF OUR DIFFERENCES?

I have always believed that to be ecumenical meant emphasizing the major dogmas of our faith, the main points of doctrine that we all have in common, and tolerating our differences. If so, aren't we in danger of polluting our faith?

* * *

Emphasizing the main principles of our Christian faith that we, Catholics, Orthodox, Anglicans and other Protestants have in common, offers a practical approach to unity and ecumenism, I agree. We share many outstanding riches: the same faith in the Holy Trinity and in Christ Jesus, the same source of graces, the same Word of God, some of the sacraments, etc. We are already united in many areas.

But our unity is imperfect. This is why we must continue to work towards total communion, if we are true followers of Christ: he really wants us to be perfectly united (Jn 17: 20-23).

Should we tolerate our differences? Maybe! As long as we don't resign ourselves to them, as long as we do not accept them as necessary. The risk would be to water down our faith and even to endanger it. True ecumenism consists precisely in affirming that to which we adhere. As we start on the road to ecumenism, we first must clearly understand and define our own faith (*Dominus Jesus*). Then, dialogue with other denominations can begin.

The entire doctrine proclaimed by Jesus is important, and the doctrinal differences between the Catholic Church and other Christian denominations are not insignificant. We must strive to discover through prayer and mutual respect what the Lord truly taught us. In this way, true work towards ecumenism will progress and, far from creating spiritual pollution, it will enrich our faith.

IS ECUMENISM LEADING US TO A NEW RELIGION?

Don't you believe that working for ecumenism creates a risk, that of starting a new religion?

* * *

I don't think so. There is no danger of falling into syncretism or an irenic solution, as long as we follow the leadership of our pastors concerning ecumenism. We find sound advice in many documents: *Ecumenism, The Code of Canon Law, The Catechism of the Catholic Church, The Ecumenical Directory* of 1993, the encyclical *Ut unum sint* published in May 1995... Our pastors are open to the action of the Holy Spirit urging Christians to work towards ecumenism. They are not afraid.

When I read about the Pope's initiatives in favor of the unity requested by Jesus, far from being anxious, I rejoice.

The Orthodox Churches remember the past and its sufferings; this adds to the theological difficulties and tends to slow down the process of union with the Catholic Church. Yet, the Holy See and the ecumenical Patriarch of Constantinople both send delegations when there are special religious celebrations. Discussions discreetly go on. The Pope has visited Orthodox countries, Romania, Georgia, Grece, etc., where he was received by the Orthodox Patriarchs.

Relations are improving with our Protestant brothers and sisters. The Pontifical Council for Promoting Christian Unity and the Lutheran World Federation, representing 124 Churches and about 60 million faithful, approved a joint declaration, in 1998, on the important doctrine of justification, salvation through grace, even though some differences remain between them. Catholics as well as Lutherans, we believe that our Christian life comes from the divine mercy, not from our own merits. Justification and salvation are free gifts of God. The document was signed on October 31, 1999, in Augsburg, Germany, where the Augsburg Confession took place in 1530 and the restoration of peace in 1555. This declaration removes almost all of the condemnations leveled by each party.

We believe that we are justified by faith in Jesus Christ; however, thanks to the Holy Spirit, we can and we must accomplish good works.

A document called *The Gift of Authority*, published by the Anglican-Roman Catholic International Commission (ARCIC) in 1999, proposes a new approach concerning the Pope's primacy and the authority; it is a step towards reconciliation and unity. George Carey, the Archbishop of Canterbury, appointed the Anglican bishop of Ottawa, Bishop John Baycroft, the permanent representative of the Anglican Church at the Vatican, so as to facilitate good relations between Anglicans and Catholics. Dialogue to discuss progress in restoring communion continued, as 30 bishops gathered in Mississauga, Ontario, in May 2000. They met again in 2001. Dominican Father Emmanuel LaPierre, associate director of the Canadian Centre for Ecumenism in Montreal, calls it a very important dialogue between such historically and theologically linked Churches.

The Declaration *Dominus Jesus*, published in Rome on August 25, 2000, on the Unicity and Salvific Universality of Jesus Christ and the Church, was criticized by Protestant Churches, but the Pope declared that the commitment of the Catholic Church to ecumenical dialogue is irrevocable. There is ongoing dialogue.

The Spirit is alive, the Spirit who is constantly building the Church.

ARE MEMBERS OF OTHER FAITHS
CALLED BROTHERS?

I don't understand the meaning the Church gives to the notion of brothers, or brethren. Are members of other faiths who worship one God called brothers? What becomes of the rest of humanity? I can't believe that God would make a distinction from the rest.

* * *

Those people particularly close to us are our 'separated' brethren, Christians of other denominations.

The Second Vatican Council invited Jewish and Christians to a 'fraternal dialogue' (*Nostra Aetate*). Are they not of a same root? Do they not have the same spiritual patrimony? Pope John Paul II, in his best-seller of 20 million copies, '*Crossing the Threshold of Hope*', explains the links that unite us to our 'older brothers', the Jewish people, to these 'beloved Jewish brothers', these members of the Chosen People. They are brothers of a particularly important title to us.

The Pope also speaks of our 'Muslim brothers', who also believe in one God. Pope John Paul II continues to speak with Muslims to remind them that they and Christians are brothers in God, that they must mutually forgive one another for past conflicts. He does not hesitate to call them 'brothers', a title that represents a new attitude, a truly fraternal overture.

Cardinal Francis Arinze wrote: "Christians and Muslims, we can collaborate to give more hope to humanity". He stated: "The relationship between us, Christian and Muslim believers, must go beyond tolerance, understood as the simple supporting of the other. For, we do not tolerate our brother, we love him".

He addressed other messages to the Buddhists on the occasion of the day of Vesakh, a day that commemorates the birth, illumination and death of Buddha. He put forth that Buddhism, like Christianity, invites one to fight evil through good, and not through violence. The words of the cardinal do not specifically mention the expression 'brother', but leave us to understand that there exists among all creatures of God, even if it is less intense, a certain fraternity.

Friendly relations with people of Hindu faith, I would even say 'fraternal', unite us equally to them and to all members of the other major world religions.

I WAS BORN OF A MUSLIM FATHER. WHAT CAN I DO?

I was born of a Muslim father and I was raised in the Muslim faith that I find wonderful when it is lived as the prophet Muhammed modeled, that is with love, humility and tolerance.

However, at the age of six months, I was secretly baptized in the Catholic Church by my godmother who is Catholic.

I am a believer in the Muslim faith but, at the same time, I love Jesus Christ. Moreover, in the Koran, he is simultaneously prophet and Word of God.

Islam is but the continuation of the messages revealed by the other prophets, Moses as well as Jesus, the spiritual Son of God. For me, going to a Catholic Church to pray or burn a candle is not a problem; in the same way as praying five times a day and fasting the month of Ramadan is not a problem.

What is essential is to have faith because, whether we want it or not, there is but one God for all, Muslim, Jewish, Christian, Hindu, etc. Salvation of man comes through his intrinsic and sincere faith.

* * *

There are many books available that could better satisfy your questions. Interfaith relationships are a fact of life in our modern world of immigration and open borders, and provokes much discussion within and among all faiths.

At the end of Ramadan, Cardinal Francis Arinze addressed a message to the Muslims: "With the other believers, we are, Christians and Muslims, 'seekers of God'". He underlined the increasing solidarity among people of our time, the desire for justice and peace, the consciousness of human dignity, the interfaith dialogue so precious to the Pope.

The cardinal wrote: "How can we not see in the dialogue among believers, notably between Muslims and Christians, a sign of hope, for the present and the future?".

All the same, one must not ignore the difference between the God of the Koran and the God revealed in the Bible. According to John Paul II: "The God of the Koran is called the most beautiful names known in the human language. However, in the final analysis, it is a God who remains a stranger to the world, a God who is only King and is never Emmanuel, 'God with us'. Islam is not a religion of redemption. It does not offer any place for the Cross and the Resurrection" (*Crossing the Threshold of Hope*, P. 153).

May a fraternal love unite believers like us, even if we cannot reconcile the differences that exist between the Muslim faith and the Christian faith, in that which concerns the Trinity, the belief in the divinity of Jesus Christ, the Word of God, the Church! We must avoid all violence and mutually respect one another.

On May 24th, 1996, the entire world learned of the news that an armed extremist Islamic group slit the throats of seven monks from Our Lady of the Atlas, in Algeria. Let us recall the witness given by their Prior, Father Christian-Marie de Chergé: "I have lived long enough to be a party to the evil that would appear, alas, to prevail in the world, and even the evil that would blindly assail me". Thinking of his impending death, he added: "That we are given to find ourselves, happy thieves, in paradise, if it pleases God, our Father of all of us. Amen! In ch'Allah".

I believe in God, in the Trinity, in the divinity of Jesus Christ, I am a Catholic Christian, but I am convinced that the Lord wants all his children on earth to live in respect and love. My response is perhaps not a direct answer to your question, but it is the one that respects your faith and mine.

I ALWAYS SAY THAT THEY WILL NEVER CONVERT ME. AM I RIGHT TO REFUSE TO ARGUE MY FAITH WITH PEOPLE OF OTHER RELIGIONS WHO COME TO MY DOOR?

I am a Roman Catholic and I often go to Church. It is against my principles to let people from other religions enter my house to talk with me. Occasionally I receive the visit of Jehovah's Witnesses. I always say to them that never would they convert me. Continue your wonderful apostolate.

* * *

I admire your Christian convictions. The Lord is with you.

To the Catholic Church was entrusted "the very fullness of grace and truth" (*Ecumenism*, No 3). Be faithful to this family of God's children to which you belong ever since you were baptized. Jesus established the Church on Peter and the Apostles (Mt 16: 18). She is Christ's Body (Col 1: 18); he laid down his life for her (Ep 5: 25).

In Christ's Church, you find pastors he himself commissioned, not pastors who commission themselves. He urges us to listen to his apostles and their successors, the Pope and the bishops (Mt 10: 14). Otherwise, we risk taking the wrong road. Unfortunately, this is what happens today to many Christians who leave the Church and no longer listen to her teaching. In many religions, the doctrine taught is no longer the doctrine Christ entrusted to his Church and her pastors.

I have written about the Jehovah's Witnesses in my first book of Christian Answers. While respecting the Witnesses and their sincerity, we may say that their religion is an "extremely dangerous travesty of Christianity", wrote Rev. Dr. Rumble, M.S.C. (*The incredible Creed of Jehovah Witnesses*). Jehovah's Witnesses predict the final destruction as imminent. Years ago, they calculated the date of the decisive battle of Armageddon (Rv 16: 16); since nothing happened when the day arrived, they decided on another date, and then another... For them, they want to convert you to their way of thinking and then send you door to door to tell others that the end of the world is at hand.

I praise you for your fidelity. To better preserve the purity of your faith, to prevent your faith from being polluted by false information, don't take any chances by listening to people from other religions who want to convert you. They are trained to make you doubt your convictions. They constantly attack our Catholic Church. They learned how to shake your faith. Do not endanger your beliefs. Rather, keep them firmly rooted by prayer, by Scripture studies, by active participation in your Catholic community.

You cannot enter into a meaningful dialogue with others unless you are well acquainted with both the Bible and the Tradition of the Church. Both of them flow from the same divine wellspring. "For Sacred Scripture is the Word of God inasmuch as it is consigned to writing under the inspiration of the divine Spirit. To the successors of the apostles, sacred Tradition hands on in its full purity God's Word, which was entrusted to the apostles by Christ the Lord and the Holy Spirit" (Vatican II, *Divine Revelation*, No 9).

I advise you not to allow people into your home whose only desire is to make you desert the Catholic Church. Be respectful, but make sure they also respect you and your faith. You can have no real dialogue with those who knock at your door; their only desire is to persuade you to join them.

HOW CAN WE, CATHOLICS, DEFEND OURSELVES?

How can we, Catholics, defend ourselves against Christians of other denominations who can quote passages in the Bible verbatim to support their viewpoint? The problem began when one of our leaders had dealings with Baptists. He was upset. He doesn't believe that the Catechism offered to Catholic children is enough to prepare them to 'defend their faith' when they reach adulthood. As Catholics, we aren't comfortable in faith discussions. I feel that we will be challenged to defend it more often in the future.

I share the concern of the leader. I believe that the answer lies in the Church offering more oppportunity to lay people so they may acquire the necessary theological knowledge. I know very little and I am nervous discussing my faith with non-Catholic friends. We need guidance in reading the Bible.

* * *

Quoting the Bible, even word for word, does not imply correct understanding. Interpretation may be fundamentalist, solely literal, with rejection of any other kind of interpretation, even if it is well-founded and legitimate. In fundamentalist interpretation, every word in the Bible is given equal value. There is an absence of intelligent reading of the text.

And also, certain religions or religious sects adopt an anti-Catholic viewpoint when they discuss theology with us, making dialogue ineffective.

In the past, seminarians studied apologetics to defend the Catholic faith against its adversaries. Lately apologetics seems to be a neglected field of study; not only could it help us strengthen our dialogue, but it would also help us to justify our Catholic beliefs in the face of ideas that are contrary to them. We must always seek to better understand the gifts of faith if we wish to dialogue with other Christians.

There are excellent Bible studies available; unfortunately the number of people taking them is small. Study material has been published on topics such as the Word of God, the New Catechism, or diverse current events. There are Catholic Information Centres with excellent resource information about our separated brothers and sisters and the beliefs they hold.

More and more Catholic lay people are studying theology, the science of God. Some are doing it by correspondence. There is no doubt that we need to work harder to understand the teachings of Christ proclaimed by our Church. Not only to be able to defend our faith but to live it more completely. Faith is upheld by the heart and action, but also by the mind.

I recommend that you read and study the *Catechism of the Catholic Church*. It is an inspired work, a precious treasure. As Catholics we believe in the Word of God as written in Scripture and orally passed down to us in the Tradition of the Church. The Pope and the bishops, successors of the Apostles, are the only ones mandated to give us authentic and faithful interpretation. They are inspired by the Spirit. If we ignore them, we will end up going in the wrong direction, listening to those who mandate themselves. The Catechism is an essential text to understand our faith.

In Catholic libraries you will find many other books to help you. Shouldn't our faith development be an ongoing process?

As a final note, it is important to join with Catholics who are journeying on a similar path, and to participate in the various movements of the Church. The Holy Spirit will help you.

- XIV -

SOCIAL LIFE

Prayer and action
Good works
Income taxes
Strikes
Globalization
How to run a business

CAN WE SEPARATE PRAYER FROM ACTION?

I don't believe in prayer without action. If we have the ability, we must help others, the sick and the disabled, or feed the hungry at shelters and daycares. It is only when I am unable to physically do so that I will simply pray for them. Am I mistaken in this attitude?

* * *

You are completely correct. Saint James wrote: "Faith, if good works do not go with it, is quite dead" (Jm 2:17).

Some people work diligently like Martha, others contemplate like Mary. Jesus doesn't scold Mary "who has chosen the better part" (Lk 10: 38-42); he doesn't blame Martha either. Our first priority is to worship God, the second is to serve others. "In so far that you did this to one of the least of these brothers of mine, you did it to me" (Mt 25: 40).

Prayer is of vital importance in our Christian lives. After that, we have a duty to help others, especially the most abandoned. Our lives have both a vertical and a horizontal dimension to them. The same is true for Jesus who spent nights praying to his Father and "went about doing good" (Ac 10: 38). He is always our example, our model.

In our hectic world, rushed and materialistic, pray often and help others, especially your children and grandchildren. Be an example.

Our bishops invite us to action. In the face of increasing negative press, we must offer our faith in Jesus Christ as a visible sign, that faith which encourages us to continue working for the betterment of our less fortunate brothers and sisters.

WHY DO WE STILL HAVE TO DO GOOD WORKS?

Jesus Christ came to redeem the world and his was the perfect sacrifice. Why then, do we still have to do good works to gain the Kingdom of Heaven?

* * *

I agree wholeheartedly that Jesus Christ came to redeem the world and that his sacrifice is perfect. Saint Paul wrote: "Christ redeemed us from the curse of the Law" (Ga 3: 13). And he wrote to Titus: "He sacrificed himself for us in order to set us free from all wickedness" (Tt 2: 14). Saint Peter said the same thing: "The ransom that was paid to free you... is the precious blood of a lamb without spot or stain, namely Christ" (1 P 1: 18-19).

Jesus, the High Priest, offered a perfect sacrifice, different from any of the sacrifices of the ancient covenant: "By virtue of that one single offering, he has achieved the eternal perfection of all whom he is sanctifying" (Heb 10: 14).

Why then, you ask, do we still have to earn our way into heaven? "Gaining the Kingdom of Heaven" is an ambiguous expression. Strictly speaking, we do not have to win this heaven which we obtain from the Lord. But we must accept the salvation and behave accordingly. Jesus said to us: "If anyone wants to be a follower of mine, let him renounce himself and take up his cross every day and follow me" (Lk 9: 23).

In-depth studies on the doctrine of justification have led to better understanding between the Catholic Church and the Lutheran World Federation. Justification by faith and then salvation by grace: such was the problem being studied.

Cardinal Edward Idris Cassidy, then president of the Pontifical Council for Promoting Christian Unity, praised the progress made through the dialogue: "This document of understanding", he maintained, "...must be considered without any doubt an outstanding achievement of the ecumenical movement and a milestone on the way to the restoration of full, visible unity..." (June 25, 1998).

Both Catholics and Lutherans believe "that new life comes from divine mercy and not from our own good qualities" (*Osservatore Romano*, July 14, 1998).

Many points require further study. Although the Catholic Church agrees with the Lutherans that good deeds are always the fruits of grace, "at the same time, ...she considers that they are the fruits of a justified person... We can then affirm that eternal life is at the same time grace and reward granted by God for good works and merits" (l.c.).

We are indeed saved by the Lord himself, but to get to heaven, we must carry out the good works which he expects of us; we must *cooperate* with grace. This is our Catholic faith. Saint James wrote that faith without good deeds is "quite dead" (Jm 2: 17).

IS IT WRONG TO OWN A HOUSE?

Is it wrong to own a house, to plan for our retirement, to wish to go on a trip? In the Gospel, the Lord tells us to sell everything that we own, to give the proceeds to the poor and to follow him.

* * *

The Church never instructed us to live without possessions, to stop being cautious in planning for the future, never to go relaxing on trips. The age of the oversimplification of the Manichaeists, of Bogomils, of Cathars, of Waldenses and of Albigensians who wish for radical poverty, is over. They were scornful of material wealth which, nevertheless, comes from God. For them, the virtue of poverty overshadowed the virtue of charity; this, the Church condemned.

One must understand the message of Christ. We must give priority to God, without becoming slaves to money. Material wealth is to serve us. A state of absolute poverty may be the vocation of some Christians who wish, in this way, to give more to the Lord. This is not a vocation for everyone.

Jesus tells us that we cannot serve both God and money (Mt 6: 24). The first Christians owned everything in common (Ac 2: 44) in a way that no one lived in misery. But the Church has never demanded that all Christians reject private possessions.

A sensible interpretation of the instruction of Christ is to detach ourselves from all material possessions; it is not necessary or even prudent to reject lawful possessions. We must also plan ahead for our children.

We read in the Bible: "Give me neither poverty nor riches, but give me only my daily bread" (Pr 30: 8).

The social doctrine of the Church teaches us to use our possessions wisely, which is the teaching of Popes Leo XIII, Pius XI, John Paul II, etc., and of our own bishops. Everyone has the right to work and to earn an honest wage. Nowadays, neo-liberalism seems to line the pockets of the rich minority at the expense of the little guy and of the countries of the Third World.

CAN I AVOID INCOME TAXES?

"Under the table? Never!", says the government.

Illegal! How else can I afford to have my apartment painted? That's how I get paid for the work I do!

How about rendering one service for another of equal value? Isn't that okay? (ex.: the mechanic who repairs his dentist's car).

* * *

I cannot resolve individual cases of conscience. I can only provide the criteria for discernment. Otherwise, the discussion would be endless.

The Lord invites to "give back to Caesar what belongs to Caesar and to God what belongs to God" (Mt 22: 21). We have responsibilities to the Lord; we must give him that which is due to him. We must also fulfill our social and civil responsibilities here on earth. We must respect just laws made by all legitimate governments. This includes taxes. Otherwise, we frustrate the government and therefore the society of which we are a part. We have our rights, but also our duties.

How can you respect the law and the spirit of the law? Can't you be guided by honest people around you and their interpretation?

We must not betray our conscience. These days, cheating seems to have become a right, as long as we are not caught doing it. News flash!... Cheating is not a synonym for honesty!

One must have respect for the laws and also a healthy interpretation. As much as it is necessary to avoid fraud, it is also important not to fall into a too strict interpretation. May your Christian conscience be sensitive without excess. You will never regret honesty and integrity.

A small friendly service rendered here and there cannot be compared with a job that is commissioned in a way to avoid the duty of paying taxes. In the latter case, would it not be seen as a type of bribe for goods or service?

WHEN THERE IS A STRIKE, WHOM SHOULD I OBEY?

We must always obey our superiors at work, but when there is a strike, whom should I obey?

* * *

We must always obey our superiors when at work..., as long as they are honest. Never when there is fraud or trickery, nor when there is danger of hurting someone.

The Church often speaks of social justice. We cannot neglect such things as social justice, human dignity, respect for other workers, or our concern for ordinary and voiceless people.

Neither should we get involved in class struggles or try to over-throw those who are in charge, without just cause. Due respect and charity are a must, especially for those who claim to be Christ's disciples.

You ask: when there is a strike, whom should I obey?

Maintain the most loyal, the most sincere and the most Christian attitude in circumstances where not everything is black and white, but where there are many grey areas.

Ask yourself the following questions for better discernment:

Is the strike legal, according to laws and conventions?

Will it improve the workers' condition?

Does it take into account, not only the particular interests of a group, but also the common good?

Is it the concern of the union leaders only?

Am I free to refuse it or not, since I belong to the union? Is my job at stake?

A thoughtful consideration of all of these questions may help you decide how to react if you should find yourself in such stressful circumstances.

CAN A CHRISTIAN REFUSE TO BE ON A PICKET LINE?

* * *

We may add this answer to the previous one.

Normally, nothing prevents you from showing solidarity with your fellow-workers by joining the picket line. Of course, you must not harm any individuals or property, even if scabs are brought in to replace you.

Trade unions shouldn't be violent. During union meetings, state your opposition to any brutality and foster peaceful discussions.

Democratic laws shouldn't be violated. Blessed Pier Giorgio Frassati, member of a trade union, can be cited as a model.

Decent laws must be honored. Our society is no anarchy. Nor do we live in a totalitarian country where opposing views are muzzled.

There is a sufficient margin of freedom for our conscience to act freely.

Again, may I refer you to the previous answer. Take into account the legitimacy of a strike, respect people and co-workers, and then exercise your personal liberty.

IS GLOBALIZATION THE WORK OF THE DEVIL?

Don't you think that the new problem of globalization is diabolical?

* * *

There is a moral globalization and an economic globalization. Moral globalization can be related to the ideal proposed by the Gospel; it started with Christ and is destined for all nations.

But, here, I'd like to write a few words about economic globalization. I don't think it's diabolical, even though the forces of evil can easily spread their venom.

Economic globalization spread rapidly after the downfall of communism. International systems of commerce and finance became universal. Capitalism triumphed.

In France, a special Commission for justice and peace published a long text on globalization, which is a new and complex phenomenon. Globalization does not have only somber aspects. Economic globalization can create greater riches with beneficial consequences.

Is the current move towards economic globalization good or bad? Will it be a new form of totalitarianism or the beginning of a new society and civilization driven primarily by high-tech first world economies? Will the market economy become the game of a few billionaires, creating a capitalist empire, a new imperialism, a cold world of gain and profit?

We must relate the Summit of the Americas, favoring free trade, with globalization. Remember the meetings of Miami in 1994, of Santiago in 1998, of Seattle in December 1999, of Quebec in 2001. The important magazine *Relations* calls such a summit "la démocratie emmurée", a walled-in democracy (March 2001, p. 10ss). A powerful resistance is organized against such neo-liberalism. Why should a strong yet peaceful opposition to the excessive power of capitalism be muzzled?

The Pope continues to denounce the extravagances of the wealthy, shown in such stark contrast against the famine and poverty in other countries. He made a bold move in asking for the remission of debts presently crippling so many nations. Facing globalization, the Church remains a ferment of peace and a leaven of international cooperation.

Globalization, good or bad, cannot be stopped, just as industrialization couldn't be halted in the 19th century. At the beginning of the industrial revolution, many feared that they would be totally replaced by machines. Some Christians, Catholics and Protestants, opposed industrial progress, while others considered it a continued creation. The same attitudes coexist today in regard to modern sciences, particularly with respect to IT (information technology).

Television and the internet open a window on the whole world. We can go window-shopping in the remote areas of the universe; it fosters globalization. The world is indeed but a village.

Christians must 'christianize' the economic globalization, and influence it particularly through NGO's (non-governmental organizations). They must make sure that governments will closely supervise globalization and pass ethical laws.

We shouldn't become fatalistic concerning globalization. We must continue our efforts to help the poorest of our society regain their human dignity. We can and must exert an influence on our politicians.

Globalization is a challenge we must face as Christians.

HOW DO WE RUN A BUSINESS IN A CHRISTIAN WAY?

I work for a commercial business in South Africa. My boss wants to direct our company according to biblical principles. What does the Lord teach about it? Can we collect tithes? Please tell me what we should do.

* * *

I presume that your boss is well intentioned and sincere. In some companies, attempts at despotic domination and total control are made in the name of false Christian principles. This might be the case if your company claims the right to tithe its employees. Tithes are part of the revenue given to the Church for its activities, according to Canon 1262: "The faithful are to give their support to the Church". The right to collect tithes belongs only to the pastors of the Church. In the Middle Ages, some noblemen claimed tithes, and the Church had to react against such an abuse.

I presume that your boss is a fervent Christian whose ambition is to run his company according to the ideals proposed by the gospels. If so, he deserves high praise. He walks in the footsteps of some well-known Christians and imitates the organizations of the 19th century: in France, Albert de Mun and La Tour du Pin; in Austria, Baron Vogelsang; in Italy, Professor Toniolo; in England, Cardinal Manning; in the United States, the Knights of Labor, etc. In the 20th century, the Catholic Unions, Confederations of Christian Workers, specialized Catholic Action and other Movements were founded on these ideals. You may recall Thomas S. Monaghan, an American who established Domino's Pizza. He sold his company and used the money to help charitable organizations; he even created an association called *Legatus* (ambassador), to invite Catholic leaders, some millionaires, to imitate him. They would be ambassadors for Christ in the marketplace and in the world.

General principles concern all Christ's disciples, company employees or not: respect for God's commandments, charity, honesty and protection of the weak and defenseless.

The Word of God should influence your company policy: "Commend what you do to Yahweh, and your plans will find achievement" (Pr 16: 3); "If you buy or sell with your neighbor, let no one wrong his brother" (Lv 25: 14).

I refer you to documents on social life published by the Magisterium of the Church: *Rerum novarum*, of Leo XIII, in 1891; *Quadragesimo anno*, of Pius XI, in 1931; three encyclicals of John Paul II: *Laborem exercens*, in 1981, reminding us that people are more important than production; *Sollicitudo Rei Socialis*, in 1987, denouncing social injustices; and, above all, *Centesimus Annus*, in 1991, underlining economic liberty and private property, and opposing unrestricted liberalism. Vatican II, in its pastoral *Constitution on the Church in the Modern World* and its *Decree on the Apostolate of the Laity*, offers practical advice and information. There are other references including the *Catechism of the Catholic Church*, declarations of episcopates, etc.

Speaking to the members of the Pontifical Academy of Social Sciences, the Holy Father desired that companies and businesses never make decisions contrary to the rights of their employees. They must allow their workers some responsibility, according to their rank. And they should do their best to create jobs, especially for the youth.

- XV -

SEXUALITY

Purity
Expressions of love
Sexual relations
Masturbation

NOWADAYS, DO WE DARE SPEAK ABOUT PURITY?

Today, priests don't preach about purity. Some seem to make concerted efforts to avoid the subject. Yet, purity is often mentioned in Scripture. Catholics should be taught about this virtue.

* * *

We must speak about purity. Jesus taught us about this virtue, necessary for Christian living. The 6th and the 9th commandments of God regarding adultery and coveting his neighbor's wife are always valid. Saint Paul wrote about those who commit certain sins and have no repentance: "You know perfectly well that people who do wrong will not inherit the kingdom of God: people of immoral lives, idolaters, adulterers, catamites, sodomites, thieves, usurers, drunkards, slanderers and swindlers will never inherit the kingdom of God... You know, surely, that your bodies are members making up the body of Christ... Keep away from fornication... Your body, you know, is the temple of the Holy Spirit... You should use your body for the glory of God" (I Co 6: 9-10. 15. 18-20).

I agree that purity must be preached with courage in order for Christians to truly love God and neighbor. The words that Saint Paul wrote so strongly in his letter to the Corinthians should be taken to heart and passed on. God's Word does not change with the times, nor is it ever out of date.

You say that you notice that preachers seldom mention God's commandments, particularly those that deal with morality. It was very different years ago, especially during Parish Missions.

I am not advocating that we should return to the age of moralism. We must remember the central reason for our existence: God's love. To speak of purity in a judgmental way may appear to violate our freedom of choice. Contemporary people are very sensitive in their autonomy. Youth has a tendency to revolt against authority. Before imposing rules, we must teach about the love of God whose laws are not arbitrary, odd, or restrictive. The Church must teach that divine laws free people and lead them to true and lasting happiness. When everyone understands how much God loves them and respects their liberty, then, in trust and confidence, they will do their best to love him in return. As God's children, they will gladly obey all of his laws, including those that concern purity.

Our pastors do speak about purity. Human sexuality is one of God's great gifts. It is not a mere 'recreational activity' that 'doesn't hurt anybody': like casual sex, masturbation, fornication (sex outside of marriage) and pre-marital sex. Such actions erode the value of marriage and of the family. Human sexuality has not only biological dimensions, but human dimensions. To learn about 'responsible sex' is more important than to learn about 'safe sex'. Man and woman were created in the image of God, not as objects to be used. We are called to live a chaste life, which requires God's help and our determination to avoid temptation and pray (Joseph Gerry, O.S.B., bishop of Portland, *Learning to love in the Lord*, 2001).

Many Christians are searching for truth and learn about purity. We must respect our brothers and sisters as they journey, "not breaking the crushed reed nor putting out the smoldering wick" (Mt 12: 20). Some of them join prayer groups, spend time at retreats, or join religious communities. Open to the Lord, they are attentive to his teaching, including his moral teachings. There are many young people who are supported by various movements and courses: youth groups, engaged encounters, marriage preparation, etc. In spite of pressures, they strengthen themselves: they pray and receive the sacraments, especially the Eucharist and Reconciliation, they practice purity.

Some people pronounce vows or make promises of celibacy; they are firm in their decision to lead chaste and pure lives. Apostles of chastity, for example Molly Kelly and Mary Beth Bonacci in the United States, speak bravely about chastity to young people. In Canada, there is the Canadian Alliance for Chastity; it is made up of different groups. Bishops constantly encourage young people to respect their sexuality.

The virtues of purity and chastity are still relevant today, even though ours is a permissive and 'feel-good' society. Purity requires decency. Modesty seems to have become outdated in our modern world. If Jansenism died during the sexual revolution of the 60's, rules of propriety seem to have also died with it. Is there no middle ground to preserve the dignity of our bodies and souls? The answer to this dilemma may be found if we increase our awareness and understanding of the virtue of purity.

WHY IS THE CHURCH SILENT ABOUT LACK OF MODESTY?

I am not comfortable with the latest clothing styles of short skirts and plunging necklines. Other than a few notices about modesty at some shrines, we rarely hear any comments by Church authorities about this increasing permissiveness. Why? Without being a puritan, my upbringing does not allow me to insult my Creator who requires me to treat my body with dignity, as a temple for his Spirit.

A woman

* * *

I congratulate you, my good lady. You are correct: the human body, for a Christian, is a temple for the Holy Spirit. You believe our bodies should be treated with dignity and refuse to wear any clothing that is overly revealing.

Without being a puritan... Society is continually changing, and fashion changes along with it. We don't need to revert to the way our ancestors dressed a hundred years ago.

Magazines, television, advertisements and movies reflect the trends of the fashion industry, and models and actors are often portrayed wearing minimal amounts of clothing or sometimes none at all! Dressing provocatively can lead to eroticism. But we are not forced to imitate what we see. You are right to wish to dress modestly. It is a pity that our morals seem to have practically disappeared. This is indeed an issue that should be addressed by priests or other Church authorities.

Shrines have a minimum dress code; not everything is acceptable. A Church is not a swimming pool where beachwear is appropriate. Simple common sense should be used. Fancy restaurants, hotels or theatres often require appropriate clothing; for the same reasons, the Church, the house of prayer, requires that everyone behaves courteously and dresses with decency.

There are often notices placed in strategic locations around many religious shrines, but the rules are difficult to enforce. In some places, such as Saint Peter's Basilica in Rome, guards are posted at the entrances to prevent anyone from entering the basilica improperly dressed. It is not always easy to do this, especially in the smaller shrines.

If anyone is obviously dressed inappropriately, the shrine officials will usually inform them. Once again, it isn't easy to draw a line between what is suitable and what is not. I agree with you that revealing tops and certain short styles are improper in our shrines.

ARE PHYSICAL EXPRESSIONS OF LOVE LIMITED WHEN WE ARE ENGAGED?

I know that it is forbidden to have sexual relations outside of marriage. Are physical expressions of affection limited even when we are engaged? We have been dating for many years and we love each other deeply. We can't afford to get married yet.

I am sure there are other couples, both young and not so young, who wonder the same question.

* * *

I am answering this question because it is a common concern. I don't want my answer to reflect any brutal condemnation of couples in relationships outside of the bond of marriage; many possess wonderful qualities. I am not here to pass judgment on consciences.

Nevertheless, I cannot keep silent regarding the laws of the Church which you have asked me to clarify. The Church laws are based on natural laws and on Revelation.

I agree with what you wrote: "It is forbidden to have sexual relations outside of marriage". According to Church law, this is called either adultery or fornication. We know that the Lord condemned adultery, the act of a married person who is unfaithful in marriage. Fornication is also condemned. "Fornication is carnal union between an unmarried man and an unmarried woman. It is gravely contrary to the dignity of persons and of human sexuality which is naturally ordered to the good of spouses and the generation and education of children" (*Catechism of the Catholic Church*, No 2353).

Cardinal Joseph Ratzinger cited the illicit nature of fornication as an example of moral doctrines that the ordinary and universal Magisterium of the Church deems to be 'definitive' teaching. "Each and everything set forth definitively by the magisterium of the Church regarding teaching on faith and morals must be firmly accepted and held" (*Ad tuendam fidem*).

Our society does not always help young people who love each other and, with respect to marriage, face financial difficulties. Obviously, in these circumstances, they must not dream of an expensive wedding, but rather of a more modest ceremony. The importance of the sacrament of marriage should convince the faithful to marry even with a minimum of funds. Consult your pastor and discuss your options with him.

While you wait, in a spirit of prayer and mutual respect, avoid any intimate gestures and settings which could put you both in peril of your chastity. Don't be tempted to have physical relations where you may lose control and lose sight of your Christian goals. If you don't want to get burned, don't play with fire!

If you truly love one another, reconsider your idea that you can't afford to get married. And, for the time being, stay faithful to the teachings of the Lord and reserve certain displays of affection until after you are married. Pray together and dream of a marvelous future where God will be an integral part of your relationship.

WHAT SHOULD I THINK OF CERTAIN SEXUAL PRACTICES?

For a married couple, are there any limits to their sexuality?

It has been the fashion of late to introduce sexual practices such as fellatio (oral sex) as healthy and even desirable with a heterosexual couple. Is there not a way to deify an activity (such as carnal pleasure) which belongs to the act of love but which is just a part of actual love?

* * *

That which you have written on the subject of love is correct. The media often present love as a mere mockery. Love is reduced to its physical aspect. This aspect deserves consideration and cannot be neglected, but it is incomplete. Love, for a human being, must not be reduced to solely a physical love which is like that of an animal.

Love is so grand. It involves all of our being in the spiritual, moral, psychological and physical dimensions. Otherwise, limited to the sexual act, it will not last, failing to come up to one's expectations, creating bitterness and messing up the best aspirations.

Love surpasses all: "Love is always patient and kind; it is never jealous; love is never boastful or conceited; it is never rude or selfish; it does not take offense, and is not resentful... It is always ready to excuse, to trust, to hope, and to endure whatever comes" (1 Co 13: 4-7). Love will never die; it is the greatest virtue. I don't see why this text from Saint Paul can't be applied to the love of a couple.

This conjugal love is a gift of oneself to the other and is open to life.

Don't be a slave to television programs or other seductive advertising which show you the exploits and acrobatics of unsatiable love in new ways. Fellatio can be allowed in a married couple if both spouses accept it and intercourse remains normal. Even if both agree to it, some actions, such as those which you mentioned, cannot be developed at the expense of a healthy understanding of human love; human love is not only physical and must remain dignified. If one partner objects to this behaviour and finds it degrading, the other must not force it upon him or her. This behaviour can become masturbation in disguise.

In conjugal love, there is a place for loving gestures, both physical and reasonable, such as sexual touching before or after the sexual act, but it must always be agreeable and harmonious. The sexual act becomes the apex, the physical ecstasy of love. It must be done in a natural way which respects the plan of God for conjugal love.

Further considerations on this matter are given in the answer to the following question.

WHAT IS ALLOWED IN SEXUAL RELATIONS?

I'd like to know what the Church says about oral sex, anal sex, the use of vibrators and other sexual 'toys'. What is allowed in sexual relations? What is sinful in intimate contact? Is circumcision necessary for a Catholic man?

P.S. I am in my twenties and I like your answers on the internet. It is a must for all youth to read them! Please answer my questions in any way possible, since I can't find a Christian answer in such fields. Thank you so much and may God bless you!

* * *

What you have written in your postscript concerning your age, on the needs of all young people, on the difficulty of finding answers on such topics, has prompted me to reply in greater detail than usual.

In today's world we are flooded with sex in advertising, entertainment and even the news. Television producers increasingly push the regulations to broadcast sexually explicit programs to a general audience at any time of the day or night, some scenes of which show perversions of nature. These days, variations on the sexual act are presented as socially acceptable, and even necessary for relationships to succeed: oral sex, anal sex, the use of vibrators, etc.

I admire your search for authentic values and your desire to know God's plan on true love.

The physical act uniting couples must be done this way: man penetrates the vagina of his spouse and ejaculates his sperm. Such is the conjugal act according to nature. Only such an act is morally good. For a Christian couple united in marriage, it becomes a sign or a symbol of God's love for us. Physical touching prior to and after the conjugal act as described above may vary according to the couple, but it is important that anything that is done is performed in mutual respect of each one's conscience.

Some gestures and actions promoted by society are disgusting to certain people; they may be completely contrary to the normal sensitivity of a young man or a young woman. Without necessarily provoking an outcry, don't some actions degrade human dignity? I leave it to you to answer.

The delicate balance of intimacy and trust between spouses may suffer if communication on this delicate subject is not open and honest.

God's plan for love and sex is good, very good (Gn 1: 31). The matrimonial alliance, which includes even sexual love, "ordered to the well-being of the spouses and to the procreation and upbringing of children, has, between the baptized, been raised by Christ the Lord to the dignity of a sacrament" (*Code of Canon Law*, Can. 1055).

Since the sexual revolution of the sixties, all taboos are gone, even those which were justified in the name of chastity and human nobility.

We must act, using our faith and our reasoning, not to condemn love and sex, but to better respect them. Love and sexuality are not simply physical; they affect our whole personality. People don't need to perform erotic feats and unnatural acts to achieve complete and true love.

As for circumcision, it is not a moral necessity for a Christian. It is a medical decision, not a religious one.

IS IT PROPER TO DISCUSS INTIMATE MARITAL RELATIONSHIPS?

What do you think about platonic friendships between men and women outside of marriage? Is it proper to discuss intimate marital relationships with someone other than your spouse?

* * *

I'd like to know how you would answer your own question...

My spontaneous reaction would be to warn you to be cautious, particularly when it's a question of revealing the intimacy of your life as a couple. What would your husband or wife think if they found out? Would you reveal that you discussed your marital problems and intimate relationship with another person, especially to someone of the opposite sex? Would your spouse be happy that you did this? This would impair your love and jeopardize all that makes you a united intimate couple. Together, you and your spouse are a unique pair. Your spouse has the right to protect his or her own privacy (*Code of Canon Law*, Can. 220).

There are exceptions in the case where a wise decision is made to undergo spiritual or marital counseling. The third party is bound by professional secrecy concerning anything that is discussed in confidence.

In this case, it is not a matter of friendship, but a necessary revealing of confidences to a specialized person. It is similar to the relationship you would have with a medical doctor.

In any case, renounce the human triangle. You would be playing with straw, which is highly flammable. To confide the intimacy of your life to a third person in the name of deepening a friendship can be used as an excuse to highlight what is missing in your life: affection, listening and dialogue. With regard to a friend of the opposite sex, this can too often fuel a destructive fire.

The heart betrays love before the body does. Without panicking, you should know to be on your guard.

ARE PRIESTS ALLOWED TO SWIM WITH WOMEN?

* * *

No law forbids it.

Priests should do what is proper, without prudishness, without prudery. However, rules of prudence and respect for convention must be taken into account; priests must avoid doing things that might scandalize normal and virtuous people.

Some people constantly watch how a priest behaves, 'trigger-happy' to point an accusing finger, skilful at damaging and even destroying reputations. Others, open-minded and accepting of all things, feel that there should be no constraints, that personal freedom is the most important consideration.

Very few things are taboo anymore; however, we haven't returned to the innocence of paradise.

Here is a summary of what Cardinal Godfried Danneels once wrote: "What we must teach our seminarians and young priests is to have a healthy lifestyle proper to those who are single. Some young priests do things married people would never do, like going on vacation to resorts where there is lack of privacy, at times where no married man would ever go. They don't see the problem. Of course, they may fall more often than they would like".

Leave it to the priests themselves to decide how they can enjoy a needed rest. Let's hope that they will respect what is appropriate and remain an example that the whole flock can follow (I P 5: 3).

WILL OUR SINS OF IMPURITY BE THROWN IN OUR FACE?

Will our grave sins of impurity, acknowledged and regretted, be thrown in our face, in front of everybody, at the general judgment, because they were not atoned for? Or else, will have God forgotten them?

When we say that God will no longer remember them, is it because they were acknowledged and rejected and that we promise never to commit them again? Is it why they will not be displayed at the last judgment? Will they be revealed or not?

* * *

We may not find an explicit answer in the Bible, but we may deduce from the Gospel that the hereafter will be much more wonderful than our life on earth. God will not have a petty-minded and revengeful look at us, forgiven sinners, and he will not allow his elect to suffer sadistic humiliation. We will be with a saving God, a loving God, a God who is anxious to treat us with kindness, like the father of the prodigal son (Lk 15: 11ss). God will not host a movie premiere of our sins and human failings before all the saints. God will not unfold the history of human depravity to voyeurs, the way some media feed voracious people with details of sexual offences.

Of course, there will be a judgment, the particular judgment after death when we encounter the Lord, and the general judgment at the end of time when the eternal celebration will begin, for all friends of God.

Nothing should be feared if we regret and acknowledge our faults. God does not take pleasure in the humiliation of his contrite children. Unrepentant sinners will be rejected by the Lord, according to Holy Scripture, but those who do the will of God will enjoy an unadulterated happiness (Mt 25: 31ss). Jesus will treat them with infinite kindness; he came down on earth, not to condemn, but to save (Jn 12: 47). After our death, he will welcome us into his Kingdom of love.

After returning to the Lord in repentance, we "need feel no shame for all the misdeeds" committed (Zp 3: 11). If our sins are forgiven, why worry? We read in Isaiah: "Though your sins are like scarlet, they shall be as white as snow" (Is 1: 18); in Jeremiah: "I will forgive their iniquity and never call their sin to mind" (Jr 31: 34); and in Hebrews: "I will never call their sins to mind, or their offences" (Heb 10: 17).

It is true that we must expiate our sins, either in this life or in the next. The Church, in her interpretation of the Word of God, always taught this truth. However, I do not believe that we should fear God's judgment when we confess our sins; God is not like us, revengeful. Again, we shouldn't be concerned.

We should feel remorse on earth because of our sins, and resolve not to commit them any more, out of respect for our loving God!

- XVI -

BIOETHICS
AND MORAL PROBLEMS

Viagra
Suicide
Assisted suicide
Abortion
Cloning
Organ donations
Anorexia
Alcohol
Fetishes
Fortune tellers

WHAT ABOUT THE USE OF VIAGRA?

Wife: *Even with medical help, my husband has become impotent. His desire is still there and he longs for caresses and pleasure. He is a very good man. Is caressing one's husband or one's wife without intercourse a sin? Is it not a greater sin to turn one's back on one's husband and not let him touch me? I don't know any more. I don't want to displease my husband or my God. What should I do?*

Husband: *I had an operation for prostate cancer that has left me unable to have normal sexual relations. I know that there are remedies now available on the market that may help me. Would I be committing a sin if I tried them?*

* * *

I will answer these two questions at the same time. They are common concerns for many people and are very delicate in nature. It would be a good idea to consult your local priest or a Christian counselor for a fair judgment on individual cases.

The mass media have extensively reported on the impotence of men in sexual relations. The recently discovered drug *Viagra* is touted as a wonder drug to cure this problem. Many people are overjoyed to have it and almost call it a miracle.

Admittedly, there are many who need medical assistance for a better sex life, and *Viagra* can now be prescribed by their doctor. There is nothing wrong with that. On the contrary! Improvement of the sex life of a couple can only make a stronger and happier conjugal and social life within the marriage. And a careful doctor will inform any user of the potential side effects with respect to certain medical conditions such as heart trouble, etc.

There are others who want to take this drug simply to increase their sexual pleasure. In this case, one must discern and choose carefully. There are limits that must not be crossed, for example masturbation for selfish pleasure. Is sex purely for recreation? Life is more than physical pleasure, and as bodies age, there are natural limits that develop. Where do we place our sexual urges within our lives? Do we give them too high a priority? Is it sex at all costs? Should couples not accept peace and serenity as the physical forces diminish?

Viagra is not necessarily the key to perfect happiness.

Let the fine threads of subtle feelings and emotions bind you more closely and grow more perfect as the years go by in your lives together as a couple. These feelings can be transmitted by your caresses and in the small ways you attend to each other's needs, as well as in your sexual relations that respect God's plan. It is only in communicating with each other, with the voice and with the heart, that each spouse will learn of the other's needs and deepest desires. There will be peace in the home and any children will develop in a healthy environment. Love will mature without spoiling. One day, your love will blossom forever.

SHOULD SUICIDES OF TALENTED PEOPLE BE REPORTED?

Nowadays, television reports more and more on the suicides of talented people who are highly regarded. Faced with this desperation of the human heart, it is certain that we must abstain from judging, as judgment belongs only to the Lord.

What can you say to people who wish to understand further?

I remember the words of Martha Robin, this mystic of our times: "Misery summons mercy".

* * *

I like that quote... Because they couldn't find encouragement and comfort, some put an end to their life. Their distress signals were not detected in time. Close friends and relatives were not able to help and guide them to centres specializing in suicide prevention.

Suicide will always be a tragedy. For us, Christians, we know that God alone is the master of our lives and that we cannot put an end to them. We also know that suffering, as painful as it can be, physical or mental, has eternal value if it is offered up along with the sufferings of Jesus. Our faith reminds us of these truths, when come the clouds and storms of life. We can be strengthened with prayer and in the contemplation of Christ who suffered for us. At the same time, we must strive to improve the palliative cares which can curb the suffering.

Suicide is not a valid solution and we must be convinced of this more than ever. Otherwise, we risk following the examples presented to us by the media. It is with a sense of responsibility that the media must talk about suicides. They must avoid presenting suicides as important news items, specifying the methods used and romancing the reason for the suicide. Otherwise, after the news is released by television, radio or newspaper, a copycat effect on the undecided is produced and cases of suicide multiply. It is inappropriate and false to say that those who committed suicide performed an act of courage; no, it is an act of weakness, that God alone will judge without doubt, and is far from being model behaviour to follow. Courage has nothing to do with it.

As the *Catechism of the Catholic Church* tells us: "Suicide contradicts the natural inclination of the human being to preserve and perpetuate his life. It is gravely contrary to the just love of self. It likewise offends love of neighbour... Suicide is contrary to love for the living God" (No 2281).

It is also written: "Grave psychological disturbances, anguish or grave fear of hardship, suffering or torture can diminish the responsibility of the one committing suicide" (No 2282). These considerations make us refrain from judging the persons who put an end to their days. They prompt us to console their relatives.

WHAT SHOULD A MOTHER THINK WHOSE SON HAS COMMITTED SUICIDE?

How should a mother react, whose son, after having planted a cross, commits suicide later that same evening? Yet, he loved the Lord. Nobody understands what happened. Whose fault is it?

* * *

Modern attitudes towards life do not help people who have suicidal tendencies or who live in anguish and pain. To solve the problem of suffering, today's society proposes an easy solution: suicide, which is contrary to natural law and God's plan. Those who commit suicide are sometimes celebrated as models of ... courage. Our Holy Father the Pope is adamantly against suicide as well as against euthanasia. Suicide, he says, "is objectively a gravely immoral action... It implies a denial of the absolute sovereignty of God over life and death".

After the tragic death of her child, it is as though a part of herself has died, and any mother would be anxious to know where to lay blame. This is the feeling of many relatives and friends of people who commit suicide. What's the purpose? It is impossible to know what is in the mind of someone who commits such an irreversible act. We can only cope as best we can with the tragedy, realizing that only God knows the answers.

This mother may find consolation in remembering her son's Christian gesture: he erected a cross for the Lord. Even though his suicide is objectively a grave fault according to the teachings of the Church (*Catechism of the Catholic Church*, Nos 2280-2283), subjectively it may not be. He died after giving a sign of his love for God; the Lord will take this into account.

We cannot judge the interior anguish which led to such an act of despair. We must commit the deceased to the infinite mercy of the Lord. May we all remain watchful in discerning signs of distress in others who may be prone to considering suicide.

MY CHILD HAS COMMITTED SUICIDE. HOW CAN I FIND CONSOLATION?

After his divorce, my son hanged himself. I always thought that God hears a mother who prays for her children. This is not true! I made three novenas. I asked God to have pity on my child and, yet, he committed suicide. Is it true that a person who commits suicide goes to hell?... He was a good man, but his wife went too far and he was fed up with everything.

I thought I was a good mother, but now I am nothing more than the mother of a man who killed himself.

* * *

I feel great sorrow for your mental suffering.

You are forever the mother of a child who is also God's child. You cannot conclude that you're not a good mother because your son lost heart and ended his life.

God alone will judge your son. God became one of us and he can easily relate to our misery and our weakness. He is a God of love who died for us; he died for your son.

You prayed. As mothers, fathers and grandparents do! Apparently, your prayer was not heard. I say: apparently..., because there is no doubt that God has taken into account your prayers and sacrifices, even if your child committed suicide. Nobody can come to the conclusion that he is damned. Of course, he made a wrong and unfortunate decision. But, was he mentally in control of the situation? Was he in full possession of his faculties? Was not his will weakened by his pain? Let's entrust him to God's love and mercy; they are infinite.

No, God wasn't deaf as you prayed for your child. Pray peacefully for the repose of his soul. Trust the Lord in his mercy and goodness.

ISN'T ASSISTED SUICIDE AN ACT OF CHARITY?

* * *

During the past years, methods of communication have diffused certain dramatic situations, some different from others: the case of Karen Ann Quinlan of New Jersey who survived for ten years after her respirator was disconnected; that of Nancy B. who asked to have her mechanical respirator disconnected and died; that of Sue Rodriguez who suffered from Lou Gehrig's disease and put an end to her days; that of Robert Latimer who caused his daughter, suffering from attacks of cerebral palsy, to die; that of Doctor Jack Kevorkian who specialized in assisted suicides, etc. The questions multiply in the field of bioethics.

We continue to kill life. Abortion is now legalized; an abortion is often called therapeutic while eliminating the births of Down's Syndrome children, etc.; this is eugenics.

The civilization of death is gaining ground in certain countries by the legalization of assisted suicides. The Pope doesn't hesitate to publicly oppose it. The Catechism states: "Voluntary co-operation in suicide is contrary to the moral law" (No 2282). Isn't assisted suicide a form of euthanasia? From an ethical point of view, it is the same thing.

Assisted suicide puts in question the value of human life. Whatever our religious opinions, we see here a moral wrong of great importance. We don't want to be taken in with misinformation, by those who want us to feel sorry for people who suffer; they present a simplistic solution. In modern times, pressure can be exerted on the sick and the aged to accept euthanasia or assisted suicide, to die 'with dignity', a very ambiguous phrase. Sometimes, the question of inheritance has a potential influence. I do not support, on the other hand, a prolongation of life, by medical disproportionate treatments. There is a difference between killing a person and letting that person die.

Saint Augustine, who died in 430 AD, wrote: "It is never lawful to kill another, even if he wishes it..." (Letter 204).

Assistance for suicide must not be decriminalized. The legalization of assisted suicide, like euthanasia, would be a serious attack on life and human dignity, as life is sacred. All the handicapped would be at risk of becoming the next victims; they would feel the tiresome pressure of society.

We must meet the new challenge of legislation concerning euthanasia and assisted suicide. It is not enough, says the Pope, to simply oppose it, but "we must also involve society and even the structure of the Church in the dignified assistance to the dying".

HOW CAN YOU EXPLAIN THE CRIME OF ABORTION?

What kind of a woman would accept to have an abortion that would prevent her from ever holding the child she carries? What kind of a doctor would commit such a murder? Why are they allowed to kill? Are they not demons?

* * *

I wouldn't say they are demons... In the *Messenger of Saint Anthony*, a pregnant mom wrote about abortion. She reminded everyone that pregnant women, especially in the first weeks of pregnancy, usually feel rotten physically and they are particularly vulnerable to people advising them of what to do (March 2001).

But, unfortunately, many people today no longer question themselves about what is right or wrong, even in matters of major importance, like abortion. Questions about abortion are becoming less numerous, since many Christians have become desensitized to this terrible crime.

Yet, such an action is clearly against nature and God's law: "You shall not kill" (Dt 5: 17). Life begins at the moment of conception and should continue till the moment of natural death.

Even politicians have no right to go against natural and divine law. They have a duty, says the Pope, "to make courageous choices in support of life, especially through legislative measures... No one can ever renounce this responsibility, especially when he or she has a legislative or decision-making mandate which calls that person to answer to God, to his or her own conscience and to the whole of society for choices which may be contrary to the common good" (*Gospel of life*, No 90).

In January 2001, Archbishop Bertrand Blanchet, of Rimouski, Canada, president of the Catholic Organization for Life and the Family, wrote a letter to the government to protest against the financing of abortions in private clinics. Abortion, he wrote, is a tragic and irreversible solution to problems. The life of the unborn child has to be protected.

I deeply admire Jim Hughes, national President of Campaign Life in Canada, Gilles Grondin, a great friend of mine, President of Quebec Campaign Life, and all those who do their very best, in the United States, in Canada and elsewhere, with all their resources and energy, to defend those who are without voice. So many others could be mentioned; God will certainly reward their efforts.

We read in a document published by the organization Priests for Life that God knows the preborn child. The Bible affirms: "It was you who created my inmost self, and put me together in my mother's womb" (Ps 139: 13); "From my mother's womb you have been my God" (Ps 22: 10). Saint Paul wrote: "God had specially chosen me while I was still in my mother's womb..." (Ga 1: 15).

"Opposition to abortion is a matter of justice and charity, and this issue is of lasting significance", proclaimed the bishops of Ontario. God has urged us to choose life and he will surely bless this endeavour.

IS CLONING PERMITTED?

* * *

Bioethics is out of breath trying to study all the problems created by the high-speed evolution of science. During the sixties and the seventies, bioethics came into being. Ever since, experts in bioethics study technological discoveries that extend beyond the field of traditional ethics and morality. Bioethics influences the creation of new ethical laws: in regard to the origin of life, its modifications, the ebb of life, death. We can easily understand the importance of religious tradition in the decision-making process involving such central life issues. Even though our pagan society snubs religious values, they must be heralded. Life received from our Creator is concerned, and so is its ultimate meaning.

According to the Pontifical Academy for Life, the cloning of animals may be legitimate and beneficial, though ethical laws are necessary for their protection. The same Academy emphasizes the difference between animals and humans. Human cloning is not the same as animal cloning. We cannot do with human beings what we do with animals. Cloning of a human being cannot be a means to attain an end.

Human cloning is not allowed; it infringes on God's rights, violates human dignity and makes use of a morally illicit technique. It distorts the human meaning of procreation. It consists in introducing an embryonic cell in an enucleated ovum, an ovum emptied of its nucleus. The new inserted nucleus must be similar to the initial nucleus in the initial egg, the zygote. The laboratory procedure reproduces an individual and makes a replica conforming to the original. But the number of embryos that are used is quite a price for such experimentation! How many embryos are frozen and destined, most of them, to be destroyed in testing and failure! The Pope was well inspired when he published *The Gospel of life* (*Evangelium vitae*), an encyclical fostering the culture of life and denouncing utilitarianism.

Cloning has not yet revealed all its secrets, or all its potential dangers! Many cloned animals died during the pregnancy or shortly after birth. According to researchers, by the time they had successfully cloned Dolly, the famous sheep, she had a chromosome age totaling her age plus the age of her sister-mother twin.

While rejecting human cloning in general, some try to justify human cloning for therapeutic reasons. The 'humanitarian' aim, that of new therapies, does not legitimatize the destruction of embryos. The generative act is not simply a technological process creating little human beings destined to be usable material. Therapeutic human cloning produces a twin child or a production in series; they are destined to provide organs and replacement tissues. They are not simple cells, but human beings who have begun their life development. They command respect, since, according to Tertullian in the 3rd century, "is already a man the one destined to be".

The problem began with the success of artificial insemination, when the act of procreation was dissociated from the expression of conjugal love. We remember the first baby born *in vitro*, Louisa Brown, in 1978. Since that time, the embryo has too often become an industrial commodity and a source of profit. In 1999, the Institute of Bioethics of the Catholic University of the Sacred Heart in Rome condemned therapeutic human cloning as an act of injustice detrimental to our dignity and civilization.

In Canada, the Catholic Organization for Life and Family, sponsored by the Canadian Conference of Catholic Bishops (CCCB) and the Knights of Columbus, studies the connection between biotechnology and bioethics. It analyses the ethical issues created by genetic manipulation. Even though the terminology is scientific and highly technical, the problems concern all of us, since they will have tremendous impact upon the future of life, of the family and of the society.

WHAT IS THE CHURCH'S POSITION CONCERNING ORGAN DONATIONS?

How does the Catholic Church see organ donation? Isn't it a wonderful gift we can offer to somebody who, otherwise, will die?

* * *

No doubt!

Developments in the field of medicine have increased the success of tissue grafts and organ transplants that have saved countless lives. The Church sees in the free gift of organs the generous action of charitable people who embrace this as another means of alleviating human misery. The Church, since Pius XII's intervention in 1956, encourages such donations without making it an obligation.

There is always a dark side to progress...: as organ transplants have become more successful, a black market has developed and in certain countries, unfortunately, organs are 'bought' from people who are desperate for money. There are unscrupulous people who even stoop as low as removing organs from street children. Human organs, including blood, should never be sold; the human body is priceless.

Nevertheless, on the whole, organ donation is a praiseworthy endeavor. In some cases, people even authorize the removal of some of their organs while they are still alive. We witness generous parents offering one of their kidneys to a child deprived of healthy ones. Of course, the Church does not condone any donation of vital organs that results in the death of the donor. In situations where the life of a donor would not be threatened and a donated organ may save someone who is seriously ill, the procedure is justified; the Pope has ratified such decisions if they are freely given.

Many people sign a donor card or some other legal agreement that their organs (heart, liver, kidneys, lungs, pancreas, etc.) or body tissue (cornea, cardiac valve, bones, skin, etc.) may be used for someone else or for medical research. Before anything is done, death must be scientifically certified. And respect must be shown for the body of the deceased.

The French bishops wrote that in the absence of a clearly-expressed intention on the part of the deceased, "it would be inhuman to remove organs and tissues if there is opposition to it, or deep repugnance or distress on the part of the family, or without their knowledge" (1993).

The free gift of organs is a praiseworthy gesture of human solidarity.

MY DAUGHTER SUFFERS FROM ANOREXIA. HOW CAN I HELP HER?

My daughter suffers from anorexia. I tried everything to help her. What can I do?

* * *

Thousands of people suffer from eating disorders: anorexia nervosa or bulimia nervosa.

Anorexia is the absence of appetite and develops especially among teenage girls and young women.

There are warning signs: weight loss, dietary changes, excessive fear of weight gain, the use of purgatives, extreme physical exercise, changes in social behavior. Their health may be permanently damaged, since the body does not receive adequate nourishment.

The causes of this disorder are not completely understood: genetic, psychological and/or neurological factors seem to be involved. There are researchers who believe that there may be some brain abnormality predisposing a person to self-starvation. Low self-esteem and other social factors are added constituents. The nervous system also exerts its influence.

The problem of anorexia has worsened with the abundance of food and our obsession with weight. Society and the mass media exert a great influence on personal appearance, and thinness is 'in'. The role models, for young people in particular, are often movie stars, sports stars and musicians, beautiful men and women who were born with 'perfect' bodies or who have had the money to pay for cosmetic changes to make them so.

Too many people suffer from anorexia. In spite of improved understanding and medical intervention, those who are trying to alleviate their suffering still don't have all the answers. Medical research continues.

Other people suffer from bulimia nervosa, which is the compulsion to overeat, or binge, followed by purging. The reasons for this disorder are similar to those for anorexia.

Parents and caregivers should never give up hope. For example, here is what one woman wrote to me... She became anorexic and looked like a walking skeleton. There was little hope that she would survive. With the encouragement of a friend, and by praying and increasing her devotion to Saint Anne, she became a living miracle and, today, she is back to her normal weight and is in good health.

I believe that faith can play an important role. We must always remember that the body is not more important than the soul. No matter what we look like, we are all God's children. This knowledge and confidence in our human dignity and our place in God's heart, regardless of our physical appearance, should reassure us and help to create the necessary balance in our psychological, spiritual and physical equilibrium.

If anyone has any concerns or questions about anorexia or bulimia, he or she should consult a doctor immediately; help is available.

WHAT IS THE ROLE OF ALCOHOL?

What is the role of alcohol in Christian life? Is drinking a good example?

* * *

Alcohol in itself is not an evil. It is how we use it that can degenerate into abuse and produce consequences of variable harm.

Everyone should be reasonable in their consumption, not only Christians.

There are many wonderful Christians who, often when in company, are able to drink a glass or two of alcohol without losing their reason or self-control.

If such dangers do not exist, an occasional glass doesn't present a problem. Saint Paul gives advice to his disciple Timothy: "Have a little wine for the sake of your digestion and the frequent bouts of illness that you have" (1 Tm 5: 23).

Alcohol abuse is always possible, especially in our society, which promotes the concept through movies and television that a social life is impossible without constantly having a glass of something in our hand. We learn by example. Drinking can easily become an addiction, particularly if it is done to handle the excess stress in our frenzied lives. It too easily can enslave us.

The results can be disastrous: messed-up personality, broken family life, traffic accidents and even death.

It is now commonly accepted that repeated excessive drinking of alcohol beverages, to the extent that the drinker's health and his or her social and family life are affected, is a symptom of serious psychological disorders. Undergoing an extensive therapy might then be the only way to recover from such an addiction.

For some people, therefore, there is only one possible solution: complete and total abstinence of all alcoholic beverages, often after a period of detoxification treatment.

We are never to cause offense to others. Saint Paul wrote: "In such cases the best course is to abstain from... wine and anything else that would make your brother trip or fall or weaken in any way" (Rm 14: 21).

Can what I write concerning alcohol be also applied to the use of other mind-altering substances such as drugs? Of course, and more so. We are bound by law to abstain from these, especially from hard drugs.

WHAT ARE FETISHES?

* * *

The word 'fetish' sounds queer to us, Christians of the 21st century.

We muse over the word 'fetish'... It seems associated with superstition and paganism. It may reflect the New Age trend. We find all kinds of websites about them on the internet. It is linked with animist cults. The word is still popular, and not only in Africa. Each one of us may have fetishes.

According to the dictionary, the word 'fetish' means objects or animals to which are attributed magic properties. Sorcerers create such objects or so design certain animals.

The Bible tells us that Hebrew soldiers were put to death for having worn objects consecrated to idols (2 M 12: 40); we may call them fetishes.

Not everything is diabolical when we speak of fetishes, but to believe in fetishes pollutes our faith.

In the erotic terminology, the word 'fetish' means inanimate objects or parts of the body, which are not sexual but are capable of becoming a stimulus of sexual desire. It could be a foot, shoes, a handkerchief, hair, the neck, etc.

Can we call amulets and talismans with alleged magic powers 'fetishes'? There are examples found in many of our homes and cars, and many individuals carry 'good luck charms' as they are sometimes called.

However, fetishes are not to be identified with the religious articles we devoutly use as physical signs of our Christian faith and helpful means for our prayer life; such religious articles have nothing magical.

What we must put aside are pagan or erotic fetishes.

MAY I HAVE MY FORTUNE TOLD WITH CARDS OR BY HAVING MY PALM READ?

When I am alone and bored, I go and have my fortune told using cards or tarots, or I have my palms read. It cheers me up to have this done. I believe the good news; as for the gloomy predictions, I do my best to ignore them.

What does the Catholic Church have against fortune-tellers? I believe that they are endowed with special powers.

* * *

It is not my place here to make a scene over what you describe as a simple hobby and pastime. To be told one's fortune by laying out cards or reading palms is quite different from participating in satanic activities: black Masses, black magic, invocation of the devil, etc. Although they are all a type of magic, we should not give each one equal weight in terms of seriousness.

At the same time, I am not saying that your activities are completely harmless nor do I condone your consultations. To be told one's fortune with cards or tarots (cartomancy) or palm reading (chiromancy), or to follow one's horoscope (astrology), all of this should be avoided because it is based on superstition. Divination can lead to fatalism, the belief that all events in life are predetermined. It is bound to influence your life and behavior, even though it might appear to be benign and innocent.

Are fortune-tellers really endowed with true gifts of knowledge and magical powers? It is possible, but far from being proven. I strongly encourage you to turn to the Lord in prayer during your lonely times rather than seeking distractions such as fortune telling.

Holy Scripture warns us: "Do not listen to your prophets, your diviners, dreamers, soothsayers, or sorcerers..." (Jr 27: 9).

- XVII -

DEATH, THE HEREAFTER

The dying
Life after death
Masses for the dead
Purgatory
Heaven

ARE THERE SPECIAL PRAYERS FOR THE DYING?

*Are there special prayers for the dying? Can we not simply re-
cite our own prayers, our rosary?*

* * *

Of course, the answer is yes. All prayer which comes from the
heart is acceptable in the eyes of the Lord. Maybe it would be good
to recite them in a low voice, in a way that the dying person might
be inspired, but without causing that person any undue fatigue.

The reciting of the occasional Our Father, Hail Mary and Glory
be to the Father can steer the thoughts of the dying person towards
God.

You may always add some invocations to Jesus, to Mary, to the
guardian angel. This traditional invocation is an example: "Jesus,
Mary, Joseph, I give you my heart, my spirit and my life. Jesus,
Mary, Joseph, help me in my last agony. Jesus, Mary, Joseph, allow
me to die in peace in your holy presence".

Better still, see to it that the dying person receive the sacraments
of Penance and of the Anointing of the Sick, if it has not been done
previously. The Anointing of the Sick is one of the seven sacraments (Jm 5: 14-15) (*Catechism of the Catholic Church*, No 1499).
Talk to the hospital chaplain or the parish priest about it.

When anointing, with oil, the forehead and the hands of the
sick person, the priest says: "Through this holy anointing, may the
Lord in his love and mercy help you with the grace of the Holy
Spirit. Amen. May the Lord who frees you from sin save you and
raise you up. Amen".

The sacrament of the sick does not cause death. On the contrary, it can return the person to health. Above all, it calms and
strengthens the sick person. The Lord continues to share in our
sufferings. He pardons the sins committed. Don't wait until the
person is near death before suggesting the reception of this sacrament.

There is still more: the 'Viaticum', in other words, the communion received to help in the journey towards God, our Father. Didn't Jesus say: "Anyone who does eat my flesh and drink my blood has eternal life, and I shall raise him up on the last day" (Jn 6: 54)?

Don't forget to visit the sick. "I was sick and you visited me", Jesus will then say to us when we will appear before him (Mt 25: 36).

MAY I DESIRE THE DEATH OF MY WIFE?

She suffers a lot and would be better off dead. We are old. She feels miserable and would like to die.

I myself suffer from many sicknesses. Still, when we look around, we see people more miserable than we are. Our life was so wonderful; this is our consolation.

Our life is coming to an end and we accept it. My wife prefers to go first, since she doesn't want to be left alone. We go to Mass every Sunday and we often pray to our loving God, to the Virgin Mary and to Good Saint Anne. We have much confidence.

Thank you for reading such a complaining letter!

* * *

You're not complaining and I sincerely admire the warmth of your love and caring.

To desire the death of somebody out of hatred or to inherit more quickly is far from being noble and Christian. But this is not your case! What you wish for is the end of your wife's sufferings. You believe in heaven after death. You accept God's will and you wouldn't do anything to cause death. I don't see how your attitude deserves any blame.

Is it not natural to wish for the end of all suffering, physical or moral, ours and that of others? Unless we turn out to be masochists or sadists!

Scientific progress is costly and health care is expensive; they prolong life and maybe also suffering. Thanks to modern medicine, people are living longer. There is increasing societal pressure in favor of euthanasia, especially in regard to senior citizens, who in turn are pressured to accept this as an option so as not to be a financial burden for their relatives and society. This is unfortunate, since the value of life and the dignity of a person can never be measured according to age or ability. Mercy killing is a crime against God and humanity.

There are those who accept and even welcome the discomforts in life so as to better imitate the suffering Saviour. They endure pain "to make up all that has still to be undergone by Christ for the sake of his body, the Church" (Col 1: 24).

This is your case. Remembering what you have received from God, you and your wife gratefully offer him what you endure. Pain has an eternal value, once offered with Christ's. Your faith teaches that eternal happiness will replace your sufferings.

You do not want your wife to suffer; you love her so much! Entrust her to the care of the Lord. You may pray that her illness and infirmities soon cease. You may hope that her life may soon end, a life that is but apparent misery. Do so in due respect to God's will. Jesus is with both of you, day after day.

IS THERE LIFE AFTER DEATH?

* * *

Yes! And this is the object of our Christian hope! One day, there will be a new heaven and a new earth. We believe in life after death, a life of utter happiness without tears or suffering. The Bible promises that there will be no more mourning or sadness (Rv 21: 1-4).

If there were no glorious resurrection, our faith would be for nothing. Saint Paul wrote: "If our hope in Christ has been for this life only, we are the most unfortunate of all people" (I Co 15: 19).

But Jesus is risen, the "first to be born from the dead" (Col 1: 18), "the first-born from the dead" (Rv 1: 5). If we walk in his footsteps and follow his way, we will enjoy the same bliss forever.

We do not believe in reincarnation; we die but once (Heb 9: 27). What we have to do is to believe in Jesus and accept him as our Redeemer. This is the teaching of Holy Scripture and Tradition. God alone can save us; we can't do it on our own.

Particular judgment will follow death, as for Lazarus and the wicked rich man (Lk 16: 19ss), and the same happened to the good thief (Lk 23: 40ss). Such judgment is final. We have nothing to fear if we have chosen Jesus, our Saviour, by our words and by our life.

If we willingly refuse Jesus as our Saviour, our serious faults will lead us to eternal damnation. Hell is often mentioned in the Bible with disturbing imagery.

Those who are saved are God's friends; yet, they may still need purification. Purgatory is no time for despair. Happiness in heaven will follow.

Heaven, hell and purgatory are dogma of our faith.

The Pope spoke about heaven, purgatory and hell. The reason for our life on earth, he said, is to enjoy full communion with God.

Is there life after death? Yes! This is what Jesus taught us: God, the God of the living, has prepared a place for us in heaven where we will enjoy peace and love and perfect happiness. It will be an eternal feast, love at first sight, love for God and for all God's children. With the *Catechism of the Catholic Church*, each of us may proclaim with certitude: "I believe in life eternal" (Nos 1020-1060).

We progress in life with the certitude that God wants all of us in his paradise. This is why we were created and why Jesus came on earth. The little grain of our human life will blossom to perfect beauty in the sunbeams of God's love.

DOES MY DECEASED BROTHER SEE ME AND HEAR ME?

I lost my brother last May. My mother is still grieving and so am I. I'd like to know if he can see me. When I speak to him in my heart, does he hear me? If I carry flowers to the cemetery, does he watch me? Is he happy on the other side? I regret not having done enough for him when he was alive.

* * *

This is a question often asked by people who mourn a spouse, a brother or a sister, a precious friend. They can't accept losing contact with the deceased.

We can trust our faith: our loved ones are not lost forever and will always live in our hearts and memories. We will all meet in heaven. Aren't we all members of a large family of which God is the Father? Aren't we all God's children, and, therefore, brothers and sisters closely united? We shouldn't doubt the existence of the communion of saints: we form God's family.

Would God break the bonds we forged together on earth? Is human friendship but an illusion?

Believe in the Lord and rely on his love. He takes good care of your relatives and friends. He allows them to be close to you, to understand your needs and to intercede on your behalf. Keep talking to your brother in your heart.

Help your brother by praying for him, since he may need to purify himself from attachment to sin. It has been written about Purgatory: "There the souls, tarnished by sin, wash themselves of their faults. Never would these souls accept to appear before God without cleansing themselves of their sins and becoming properly attired. They gladly accept to do so in Purgatory. Let's pray for them, in order to help them".

After someone dies, people often feel regret that they didn't do more while they were alive. No need to despair! They can make up for it through prayer. Let them devote more energy helping those who are still living around them. Life goes on...

TELL ME WHY, WHEN I PRAY TO MY DEAD HUSBAND, HE DOES NOT ANSWER ME?

You are a priest and you know more than I do. Tell me why, when I pray to my dead husband for favors, he does not answer me? Yet, I know he is in heaven! I have asked him for good health, and to be on good terms with our children.

* * *

I receive many questions along similar lines. People ask questions about praying to the saints, the Virgin Mary, and even directly to Jesus. They have prayed and not seen any results. They then conclude that the prayers were useless and it seems to them that God does not really exist.

Too often, they pray as though prayer is a magical formula for obtaining grace from heaven: employment, healing, better health, money, peace in the household...

It's as though everything should be given to them automatically... 'I pray; therefore I will receive such and such a benefit'. This is a wrong idea about God and about prayer.

God will never give us anything that will harm us, nor anything that will remove us from our human condition. He always grants us gifts that will truly help us. He responds to our prayers in a way that leads us to true happiness. He guides us in the direction of heaven. "What we suffer in this life can never be compared to the glory, as yet unrevealed, which is waiting for us" (Rm 8: 18).

In his moment of agony, Jesus prayed to his Father to be released from the cross and from death. Apparently, his Father didn't listen to him; he did not take away the cross. Yet, he "glorified" his Son (Jn 17: 1). As for ourselves, we continue in "sharing his sufferings so as to share his glory" (Rm 8: 17). We must follow Jesus, carrying our crosses behind him, our individual crosses of suffering and deprivation (Lk 9: 23).

Even as Christians, we can never stop being human, with our sorrows and our joys. But we have faith and we know that everything happens to us for the greater good. God, who loves us, walks beside us, helping us to find our way to heaven. Trust in him!

ARE MASSES FOR THE DEAD NECESSARY?

It is said that when we die, our destiny is fixed; we are either saved or we are not. I really feel that the offering we give to have a Mass said for the deceased only benefits the person to whom we give the money. I believe that the teaching of the Church on purgatory is an invention of the clergy.

If our destiny is predetermined, no matter how many Masses are said after we are dead, it will not change anything. What is your opinion?

* * *

My opinion reflects the thinking of the Lord and of the Church. If other people, who do not share our faith think otherwise, they are free to do so, free to attack the Church, her doctrine and her Tradition. But my faith regarding eternity will never change.

Heaven, hell and purgatory exist; they are faith dogmas. As soon as we die, we go before God for particular judgment. According to the way we lived, we will either enjoy eternal happiness or be forever deprived of it. Our fate, as you say, is indeed fixed when we die.

If we are rewarded with eternal happiness, we may experience the purification of purgatory before the joy of heaven. This is the Church's teaching based on the Book of Maccabees in the Old Testament. We read that pious Jews, believing in the resurrection, took up a collection to make a sacrificial offering for the dead, and that they prayed for them, that they be delivered from their sins. The Bible says: "...The thought was holy and devout" (2 M 12: 43-45).

The Church, inspired by the Holy Spirit, decrees that we too should help the dead through our prayers, especially in the great prayer of the Mass, that they may be delivered from their sins. This practice, based on the Word of God (v.g. 1 Co 3: 15) has been followed by the Church since her origins. She has not changed (*Catechism of the Catholic Church*, Nos 1030-1032). We can also help the deceased by doing good works and through indulgences.

IS IT NOT THE RESPONSIBILITY OF THE SOULS IN PURGATORY TO MAKE AMENDS FOR THEIR OWN SINS?

They say that we must pray for the dying and poor souls in purgatory. Is it not their own duty to expiate for the sins they have committed? God has given them liberty.

* * *

First a word on purgatory... The Pope wrote the following with regard to purgatory: "All trace of attachment to evil must be rejected... Purification must be complete and this is precisely what is the object of the Church's doctrine on purgatory... Those who, after death, live in a state of purification are already in Christ's love, who frees them from what remains imperfect". This is the teaching of the Councils of Florence (1438-1445) and of Trent (1545-1563). The Lord, in his kindness, purifies us so as to unite us to him more closely. This consoling doctrine is opposite to that of reincarnation, which implies that our souls will continue their earthly and imperfect existence, hoping that their futile efforts will help them. The Curé of Ars said: "Purgatory is the good Lord's infirmary". There we find God's friends, happy being saved by him.

No doubt the souls in purgatory must pay the penalty for the faults they voluntarily committed before the end of their life on earth. But is it not an act of charity to help them if we can?

If you have children, you do not hesitate to go to their rescue if they get into trouble, even if you know that they alone are responsible for their problems.

Justice seeks punishment for the guilty, without the possibility of outside help. Charity, love and mercy differ from justice.

Our prayer for the deceased is based on the doctrine of the mystical Body of Christ: we have the power to help one another. The Church always taught about the 'communion of saints', that is, the friendship binding together all God's friends, those in heaven, those on earth and those in purgatory. We pray for those who will soon appear before God. We offer Holy Mass, the great Eucharistic prayer, for the souls in purgatory, particularly for those we have known and loved on earth. They themselves pray for us.

We form a loving family whose members are happy to help one another.

IF RELATIVES ARE DAMNED, HOW CAN WE BE HAPPY IN HEAVEN?

If, among those whom we have loved on this earth (parents, spouse, children, etc.), some are damned, how can we be happy in eternity?

* * *

Life after death is not the same as the life we live today. Heaven far surpasses our limited earthly conceptions. God alone can respond to this question and the answer, I am certain, will exceed our expectations. It will satisfy our profound desire to be happy without being compelled to agonize over the fate of other souls whom we have so loved on earth.

What is heaven? Is it not the sight of God, a face-to-face meeting with infinite Beauty, Goodness and Love? Is it not the sharing of the happiness of God himself, a sharing in the joy of the Trinity? Is it not having a place in the glory and the gladness of Christ resurrected? We will find eternal life and unlimited happiness in God.

Jesus did not provide us with the specific details of what is beyond our understanding. According to Saint Paul: "We teach what scripture calls: the things that no eye has seen and no ear has heard, things beyond the mind of man, all that God has prepared for those who love him" (1 Co 2: 9).

Of course our limited and cloudy minds have difficulty imagining heaven. We do not have to be overly concerned. Our loving God would like to see us all with him. He cannot stop loving us, even when we transgress, even when we are damned. It is not him who rejects us, it is we who freely reject him.

I cannot give you a more precise answer than this. I trust in the Lord of all justice and all mercy, that he will grant us, both you and me, eternal happiness, that he will come to the aid of all those who make their way on this earth, those whom we love and whom the Lord also loves. He died for us all, sinners. Let us try hard to love him. Our love for him will be reflected on those whom we love, thanks to the communion of saints. Our love for God will be for them like a cleansing blessing from God.

I have confidence in him, and I pray to him, for myself and for those I love, that one day we might experience together the heaven of God. And we cannot judge the depths of the hearts of our deceased. Our happiness in heaven will be untroubled.

HOW CAN GOD CREATE HUMAN BEINGS THAT WILL BE DAMNED?

How can a God who is omnipresent, omniscient and infinitely good, create human beings that will be damned? In other words, if he knows everything from the beginning to the end of time, then he must also know that certain people will be damned. Why, then, did he create them in the first place?

* * *

We have neither God's wisdom nor his infinite knowledge, but we have every reason to believe that he is infinitely good.

The human limitations of our reasoning make it difficult to reconcile God's love with his justice, and human freedom with grace and predestination.

God creates us out of love. Through his love, he redeems us. Through his love, he gives us grace. He loves us enough to allow us freedom and he never forces his love upon us. He respects our choices; we are his children, not programmed robots. We have only to blame ourselves if we prefer to remain distanced from his love and the happiness he offers us.

There is certainly a mystery in all this... We must respect God and trust in him.

Great thinkers throughout history tried in vain to scrutinize God's plans. Among the more well known, there is Saint Augustine, who had abundant firsthand knowledge regarding human frailty, the Dominicans and Jesuits, who tried to intellectually define grace and freedom, and Luther, who anguished over his salvation. The austere Jansenists stressed human efforts and the passive Quietists divine love. The question remains unresolved even today: How do we reconcile the love of God and the help of his graces with human freedom and sin; how could he create anyone who would end up in hell?

In full knowledge that we might possibly reject his love, God creates us all as free human beings and then offers us eternal happiness, the true happiness with him, showing us the way and offering to lead us. How can we find fault with such love? "But who can give lessons in wisdom to God?" (Jb 21: 22). "Yahweh, what variety you have created, arranging everything so wisely!" (Ps 104:24). We can only affirm that God's "understanding is beyond fathoming" (Is 40: 28).

Let's never forget God's infinite love and mercy. "For it is with Yahweh that mercy is to be found and a generous redemption" (Ps 130: 7).

- XVIII -

THE END OF THE WORLD

Days of darkness
The Antichrist

THREE DAYS OF DARKNESS BEFORE THE END OF THE WORLD, IS THAT TRUE?

I visited your site on the internet and I was very surprised. I had a lot of questions and, thanks to your web page, I found many answers.

I heard there will be three days of darkness at the end of time... And a lot of other things will happen. But, is it true? It's hard to believe. I have also heard that the end of the world is very near. Everything will begin with the coming of an asteroid, which will hit the earth. This would be followed by three days of darkness, and the arrival of space ships to save us. At the end, all humans will come back on a new earth; all will be happy; there won't be any more violence, any more war, any more unhappy people, any more suffering... A real fairy tale!!!

Didn't the Virgin also foresee terrible events? Does the Church mention it? Will this really happen?

A worried girl searching for the truth

* * *

Don't pay any attention to such idle gossip which is commonplace every time there is a calamity and especially today as we begin the new millennium.

There are always prophets of gloom. They announce apocalyptic events, frightful catastrophes which will soon mark the end of time. Some of them falsely claim that some prophecies come from the Virgin Mary. Father Jozo Zovko, the parish priest of Medjugorje when the apparitions first took place, says that nothing could be more contrary to the Medjugorje message than this climate of violence and fear. The *Gospa*, he says, the Virgin, never inspires terror and panic! She is the Queen of Peace who never threatens her children with wars and disasters; she radiates love and calm.

Prophets of woe speak of days of darkness. These days, they say, will be followed by a period of peace, a terrestrial reign for the

Messiah, a return of the lost paradise, one thousand years of happiness: millenarianism.

Such fundamentalist ideas are inspired by a literal interpretation of the Bible, particularly of the Book of Revelation (Rv 20: 4).

Such rantings are nothing new; they have always existed in the Church, with those who were easily influenced by their fearful imagination as they faced the future.

What does the Church teach about it?

The Church believes that before the second coming of Christ, a final trial, which will shake the faith of numerous believers (Lk 18: 8), will occur. Jesus said: "Many false prophets will arise; they will deceive many, and with the increase of lawlessness, love in most men will grow cold; but the man who stands firm to the end will be saved" (Mt 24: 11-13).

The Catholic Church, as well as the Protestant Churches, rejects millenarianism, a thousand-year peace on earth, which would be due to Christ's intervention. For the Catholic Church, this idea misleads us as to what the Kingdom is (*Catechism of the Catholic Church*, No 676). It would be "a falsification of the Kingdom". Reject then the theory of three days of darkness followed by a period of peace. This belief is not taught by the Church, and the Pope never mentions it.

Christ already reigns on earth, thanks to the Church. The Lord's reign will never be complete till he comes in glory, which will be after a final assault by the forces of evil (Lk 21: 27). The return of Christ, at the end of time, will be the moment of the final judgment and of the definitive triumph of good over evil (*Catechism of the Catholic Church*, No 681).

Let nothing destroy or falsify our Christian hope!

MUST WE BELIEVE IN THE ANTICHRIST?

We hear more and more about his coming and the second coming of Christ in our time... How do we prepare for it? What are we to think of the people buying blessed candles for the predicted days of darkness?

With all the recent natural disasters like floods, ice storms, tornadoes, etc., we are told that the end of the world is near. How do I help my friend understand that it may still be a long time from now?

* * *

The Antichrist will come before the return of Christ. He will oppose Christ and his reign. The Antichrist, says the Bible, confronts God; he denies the Father and the Son (I Jn 2: 22).

Each century has known its share of ecological disasters, calamities and human destruction. When these happen, there are those who are quick to announce that the time of the Antichrist has come, that the end of the world is here.

It is the same attitude these days. Nuclear threats, menacing clouds on every horizon, appear ready to drown us with torrential evil; humanity is threatened. Devastating natural phenomena and horrendous wars continue to happen; they make news headlines as soon as they occur. Some would say that these disasters are a foreshadowing of the end of time. And especially as we enter a new millennium, there are more and more 'prophets' of gloom.

The Antichrist will come; he is here already. He, the Rebel, will be manifested before the coming of the Lord in glory (2 Th 2: 1-12). "Rebellion is at its work already, but in secret" (2 Th 2: 7). However, we must not allow ourselves to become alarmed in thinking that the day of the Lord is here (2 Th 2: 2).

Who is or who will be the Antichrist? Saint John writes: "Now several antichrists have already appeared" (I Jn 2: 18); "There are many deceivers about in the world, refusing to admit that Jesus Christ has come in the flesh. They are the Deceiver; they are the

Antichrist" (2 Jn 7). The Antichrist is and will be the Seducer par excellence.

Let us not panic. "Be brave: I have conquered the world" (Jn 16: 33).

The end of the world, says the Pope, is "already a reality beginning with the historic coming of Christ". This coming is present and future. The Pope adds these significant words: "Christ has not fixed a time and day for his glorious return. Do not let yourselves be troubled with illusive dates and let us keep our trust".

INDEX

A

Abba: 21, 23, 25, 120

Aboriginals: 55

Abortion: 44, 139, 153, 222, 227, 228, 229, 230, 232

Abraham: 19, 32

Abstinence: 71, 72, 229

Abuse: 44, 55, 77, 92, 103, 109, 115, 204, 227

Ad pascendum: 107

Ad tuendam fidem: 204

Adam: 19

Adopt: 111

Adultery: 35, 109, 110, 200, 204

Africa: 53, 58, 196, 228

After-life: 18

Agnosticism: 20

Agreda (Maria d'): 141

Akita: 132

Albigensians: 190

Alcohol: 45, 47, 227, 228

Alcoholics Anonymous: 45

Algeria: 56, 181

All Saints: 65, 139

All Souls' Day: 139

Allah: 34, 135, 181

Alliance: 111, 112, 128, 201, 207

Alphonsus of Liguori (Saint): 126

Ambrose (Saint): 53, 129, 130

American Secretariat for the Liturgy (The): 88

Anal sex: 206, 207

Angels: 43, 143, 144, 145, 146

Anglican Church: 178

Anglican-Roman Catholic International Commission: 178

Anglicans: 22, 175, 176, 178

Anne: 28, 29, 114, 121, 135, 139, 140, 141, 142, 143, 166, 226, 233

Anointing of the Sick: 73, 115, 232

Anorexia: 225, 226

Anti-Semitism: 56, 58

Antichrist: 39, 248, 249

Antilles: 53

Apartheid: 58

Apocalypse: 38, 39

Apocryphal books: 140

Apologetics: 184

E

F

262

Religious: 25, 34, 46, 54, 56, 58, 59, 66, 68, 71, 74, 77, 87, 102, 103, 105, 108, 132, 141, 158, 159, 160, 168, 172, 177, 184, 201, 203, 208, 219, 222, 229
Remorse: 85, 86, 93, 211
Rerum novarum: 197
Resurrection: 19, 26, 68, 69, 81, 98, 99, 125, 138, 181, 234, 238
Revelation: 19, 21, 22, 38, 39, 132, 133, 134, 150, 204, 247
Robin (Martha): 215
Roman Congregation for Institutes of consecrated life and Societies of apostolic life: 160
Roman Empire: 23, 38, 53, 77, 170
Roman Missal: 96
Rome: 38, 39, 59, 66, 67, 89, 92, 168, 172, 173, 178, 203, 223
Rosary: 50, 118, 134, 135, 136, 232
Rushdie (Salmon): 34

S

Sabbath: 35, 36
Sacram unctionem infirmorum: 115
Sacrament of the sick: 114, 115, 232
Sacramentals: 73, 74
Sacraments: 51, 61, 65, 72, 73, 74, 81, 89, 99, 113, 115, 125, 132, 161, 175, 176, 201, 232

Sacred Heart: 60, 223
Sacred Penitentiary: 88
Sacrifice: 100
Sacrum diaconatus ordinem: 107
Saint Anne de Beaupre: 28, 58, 125, 142, 143
Saints: 52, 53, 61, 65, 75, 77, 83, 86, 87, 91, 118, 119, 122, 128, 130, 132, 139, 140, 146, 152, 161, 163, 210, 236, 237, 241
Salvation: 19, 32, 80, 83, 84, 100, 125, 128, 129, 135, 144, 145, 146, 161, 175, 177, 178, 180, 189, 242
Sanctifying gifts: 165
Sappier (Father Curtis): 143
Satan: 38, 144
Savior: 28, 38, 43, 44, 85, 126, 129, 140, 146, 163
Schisms: 58
School: 46
Scripture: 25, 28, 32, 33, 37, 130, 144, 145, 146, 149, 164, 175, 183, 185, 200, 211, 230, 235, 241
Scruples: 162, 163
Seattle: 195
Second Vatican Council: 96, 167, 179
Sects: 82, 172, 173, 184
Secular institutes: 159
Secularism: 34, 61
Secularization: 60, 61
Seder: 68
Sermon on the Mount: 36, 109
Sexual relations: 203, 204, 206, 214, 215
Sexuality: 111, 201, 204-208

Printing Press: Imprimerie Le Renouveau